Build a Better Brain: Using Neuroplasticity to Train Your Brain for Motivation, Discipline, Courage, and Mental Sharpness

By Peter Hollins,
Author and Researcher at
peterhollins.com

Table of Contents

Build a Better Brain: Using Neuroplasticity to Train Your Brain for Motivation, Discipline, Courage, and Mental Sharpness 3

Table of Contents 5

Chapter 1. Neuroscience, Plasticity, and the Changing Brain.. 7
Phineas Gage: The Case of the Pierced Brain 12
The Phantom Limb Phenomenon 17
A Primer on Brain Structure 25
Brain Structures in Neuroplasticity............. 31
The Triune Brain Theory............................... 41

Chapter 2. Plasticity in All Forms: How Does the Brain Change? 50
What Is Neuroplasticity?............................... 58
The Process of Neuroplasticity 63
Primary Aspects of Neuroplasticity.............. 72
From Synaptic Pruning to Neurogenesis...... 76

Chapter 3. Principles of Neural Growth..... 83
Principle #1: Stimulation Is Key 90
Principle #2: Enrich Your Environment......101
Principle #3: Be Methodical, Persistent, and Repetitive 107
Principle #4: Take Care of The Engine 111

Chapter 4. The Neuroscience of Yes and No
.... 129

The Neuroscience of Yes: Motivation,
Discipline, and Focus......................................133
The Inhibition System 146
The Neuroscience of Pumping Yourself Up.150
Visualization: Seeing Is Believing 155
The Neuroscience of No: Fear and Anxiety .164
Rewiring the No Response...........................178

**Chapter 5. Creating and Breaking
Unconscious Habits 193**
Habits and the Brain 196
Hebb's Axiom 202
Addiction and Neuroplasticity 205
How to Build (or Break) Habits....................208
The If-Then Technique..................................220
Common Pitfalls to Habit Formation...........227

Summary Guide... 238

Chapter 1. Neuroscience, Plasticity, and the Changing Brain

When we say somebody's got a "great brain," we're probably referring to their intelligence or smarts.

If someone figures out a complex math problem, they've got a "great brain." If they decode the hieroglyphics on a cave wall with great ease, they've got a "great brain." If they can finish a *New York Times* crossword in record time (or at all, frankly), they've got a "great brain."

Is it accurate to say that these accomplishments are actually a reflection of their actual, physical brains?

Well, everything we do—what we think, what we say, how we behave, and what habits we develop—springs from the complex biological processes of the brain. In fact, the brain is the center of the human. Even what we perceive as non-mental experiences and sensations—like hunger and pain—are dictated by neurobiology. Things like physical activities, emotional reactions, pain, or sensory development are all controlled and dictated by the brain. People with better memories tend to have larger hippocampi, and singers tend to process the act of imitation better than those who cannot sing. All of who we are comes from the unique way our individual brains have developed.

Suffice to say, it *is* an accurate statement that someone's high-functioning and intelligence (or lack thereof) is certainly a result of the structure of someone's brain. "Great" on the other hand is a matter of subjectivity. But as you will read, it is an indisputable fact that everyone's brain is wired differently, from things as innocuous as childhood habits to the environments they were exposed to the prior week. It certainly doesn't make someone's brain inherently *better* than others, perhaps simply better suited for specific purposes.

Luckily, we aren't slaves to the brains that we were born with. If that were true, no learning would ever be possible, and it's quite unlikely you would be able to even read this sentence. Not everyone has equal potential in any pursuit; some people might be born with a greater propensity for music, for instance, or learning new languages. But the brain is always changing, and "great" takes on a wide range of definitions and metrics. Most of the time, "great" just means practiced or made habitual over a longer period of time.

The brain goes through actual physical alteration whenever we learn a new fact, make a new memory, or meet a new person. It's how much our individual brains are accustomed to changing, adapting, shifting, and creating connections that determines how "great" we function and are able to achieve our goals.

We call this adaptation and growth *neuroplasticity*: the ability of the brain to change itself in response to the stimuli it encounters. You can imagine this to be the cornerstone of learning, memory, self-discipline, habits, and even motivation. With neuroplasticity, you set your own potential; without it, you are destined to have a brain set in stone. The ability of our brain to change and adapt is truly what makes us unique as a species.

This proposition naturally leads to a near endless set of questions.

- What is actually happening in the brain when we learn or create a new habit?

- What does neurological change actually *do* to us on a physical and biological level?

- How does neuroplasticity work—for better and for worse?

- Is neuroplasticity something that just happens to us, or is it something we can control to make positive changes in our lives?

- And of course: "I have a really big head. Does this mean I am destined for great things?" (This particular question is easily answerable: unfortunately no, because that is the fallacy of engaging in *phrenology*, which is a centuries-old practice of predicting someone's temperament and intelligence based on the shape and bumps of their head. This can be lumped in with the likes of bloodletting and lobotomies in terms of *questionable* medical effectiveness.)

This book answers all of those questions. In addition to providing important background to understand yourself and your brain, you will read about exactly the steps to take to develop yourself in just the way you want. Let's face it: not everyone was born with a "great" brain, at least in the areas that we want. I would have loved to be better at math, for instance, and others have developed nasty habits that hold them back from happiness. It's now time to learn how you can make neuroplasticity work for you, and grow beyond what you were born with.

Phineas Gage: The Case of the Pierced Brain

In order to better understand how the brain works, it will be helpful to learn about one of the seminal cases in neurobiology, which happens to be the one that definitively tied physical brain structures to specific mental functions. The intriguing case of Phineas Gage allowed scientists to make a correlation between something tangible and what was thought to be ethereal thought and consciousness.

For centuries, scientists, psychologists, and philosophers have debated the origins of emotions and personalities: what creates and triggers them and how they are regulated. Significant progress in this field came in the aftermath of an unfortunate— and, fair warning, somewhat graphic— accident that happened in 1848.

Phineas Gage worked as a foreman for a construction team working on a railroad bed in Vermont. It was not gentle or safe work. Gage's crew used explosive powder to blast away rock that needed to be cleared for the tracks. The gunpowder needed to be tamped, or lightly packed, to concentrate its power, and this was accomplished using an iron tamping rod about three and a half feet long and weighing over 13 pounds. You might be able to see where this is going.

On September 13, Gage was tamping the gunpowder with the tamping rod when it suddenly exploded right from under him. The tamping rod shot up like a javelin and pierced Gage's left cheek, tore through his brain, blasted out the top of his skull, and landed approximately 30 yards away from Gage. Gage was left with two literal holes in his head and yet was otherwise, well, *relatively fine*.

Gage survived and was even able to communicate with attending doctors that afternoon. Historians believe he might never have even lost consciousness during the incident, even though the left part of his frontal lobe had been ripped to shreds.

He did eventually lapse into a coma, during which doctors assumed he was about to die. However, Gage eventually woke up, recovered his physical strength, and was able to go back to work (though not, obviously, at the railroad) mere months after the accident.

The shocking accident and Gage's remarkable recovery might be legendary strictly on their own merit—but they also proved to be one of the most significant developments in the history of neuroscience.

Did we discover that people walk amongst us with superhero-like healing abilities? Not quite.

After the accident, Gage's workers, family, and friends described a significant change in his overall personality. Although no specific records exist pertaining to how they regarded Gage before the catastrophe, afterward his friends and associates generally agreed that he was formerly friendly, good-natured, and hard-working. But after the event he became ill-tempered and frequently drank. He became a braggart and made shocking sexual remarks without thinking. He lacked a sense of social inhibition that would have prevented him from being, to put it bluntly, a jerk. He was for all intents and purposes an entirely different person.

But Gage's evolution into a despicable human being turned out to be a huge turning point in the study of brain science.

Gage's case was the first that, more or less, proved the brain's role in personality. Neurobiology was still a new science in the nineteenth century, and scientists during Gage's lifetime were only beginning to understand the brain's role in someone's intelligence, personality, character, and overall behavior. The dramatic change in Gage's disposition—even as his intellect and work ability were, comparatively speaking, intact—inferred that the brain, especially the frontal region, is tremendously important in forming personality. These findings dramatically altered the course of neurobiology. Studies from this century have confirmed this conclusion beyond a doubt—the frontal cortex is pivotal in personality, inhibition, decision-making, and social functionality. Of course, scientists were also able to infer that no vital functions were contained in the frontal region.

In 2004—150 years after Gage's death—scientists from UCLA reconstructed his skull using digital imaging. They found that his injuries might have been more extensive than initially realized: approximately 4% of his cerebral cortex had been destroyed, along with about 11% of the white matter in his frontal lobe. They also determined severe damage had come upon the connections between Gage's frontal cortex and his limbic system. Put simply, Gage underwent a left frontal lobotomy (in the worst way imaginable).

More centrally to the purpose of this book, Phineas Gage is a striking example of just how adaptable and changeable the brain is. It can suffer a dramatic physical change, and those changes can result in modifications to one's personality.

Of course, doctors overwhelmingly advise *not* trying to effect brain changes the way Phineas Gage did. But it's clear that the brain is malleable, and that if one went about stimulating certain brain regions in a more *convenient and beneficial* manner, it's a natural conclusion that you can alter aspects of your personality and even intelligence as well.

The Phantom Limb Phenomenon

Further indication of the brain's complexity and fantastic adapting ability comes from examinations of an odd phenomenon that affects amputees: the *phantom limb*. This is a curious condition experienced by an estimated 60–80% of all amputees—the sense that the limb that's been removed is actually still there—hence the term phantom.

Someone with the phantom limb sensation feels that their missing appendage is still fully functional: making gestures, itching, and twitching as if it were still there. The sensation can even be *painful*, especially if the limb was accustomed to being in pain or was lost in a painful manner.

In trying to alleviate the pain of a phantom limb—which of course can't respond to traditional pain medication since, well, it's not there—scientists discovered that the phenomenon is directly related to brain structure and function. The brain has an amazing ability to compensate, repair itself, and adapt—and when you lose something as significant as a limb, curious things start to happen in the process of repair.

As with the science behind the Phineas Gage incident, knowledge about the cause of the phantom limb has evolved as we've learned more about neurobiology.

At first scientists theorized that the phantom limb was caused by irritations in nerve endings that were cut during amputations. The severed nerves were, according to this theory, sending messages to the brain that it couldn't decipher—so it rendered them as "pain." Doctors used this theory to guide their treatments of those with phantom limb, many of which included *additional* amputation to remove the theorized irritated nerves.

This method actually resulted in the patient feeling *more* pain, and it also gave them yet another phantom limb to contend with. In hindsight, this is the equivalent of trying to even out a haircut to the point where there's no hair left at all.

Another (somewhat dismissive and insensitive, if you ask me) theory was that the amputees simply *missed* their limbs and were subconsciously trying to wish them back into existence. Canadian psychologist Ronald Melzack introduced the theory of the "neuromatrix" in 1990 in an attempt to explain the origin of phantom pain. Melzack believed that the structure of our brain's neural networks coordinates all the sensations that human beings feel.

Modern research on phantom limbs centers on the primary somatosensory cortex (PSC). This part of the brain manages and processes all of the sensory input the body receives, from the five senses and also pain, warmth, body position, and so forth. The PSC also contains a very precise neural "map" of all body parts and the nerves that represent them—there are specific locations in the PSC that correspond to specific body parts. Based on the information the PSC gets, it processes all the sensations the body feels.

Neuroscientist Vilayanur Ramachandran was the first to theorize that the PSC played a major part in the phantom limb phenomenon. In experimental trials, Ramachandran discovered that the PSCs of amputees get dramatically restructured, and in fact the sensory map of the brain gets rearranged and distorted to compensate for the damage and lack of sensory information from the missing limb. In other words, the brain began to assign sensations from other parts of the body to the missing limb. This finding pointed to a link between phantom limbs and the brain's plasticity—its ability to change itself.

This process is known as *cortical remapping* and is perhaps best explained using a visual tool invented by Dr. Wilder Penfield and called the *homunculus*, which is Latin for *little man*.

The homunculus represents the brain as a human being, terribly distorted as the size of various body parts are sized according to how many nerve endings are dedicated to them and how complex they are. The hands, lips, and genitals, for example, are greatly oversized on the homunculus because they have a wider range of sensory input (such as motion and touch) than, say, the shin or back. The homunculus might look like some sort of gremlin, but it illustrates the PSC neatly.

Now, imagine that you are packing the homunculus into a suitcase. It would be folded over itself, and random body parts would be stacked and touching. The homunculus's head might touch the knee, and the hands might touch the toes and ears simultaneously.

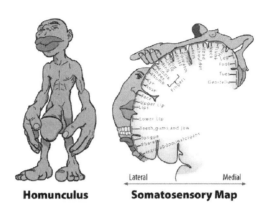

Homunculus   **Somatosensory Map**

Image courtesy of ResearchGate

The homunculus helps to explain phantom limbs because even if a body part isn't there, the brain still has a space reserved for its sensory inputs. And in its normal course of duty, if that space reserved for a certain body part isn't used, inputs from neighboring parts of the homunculus packed into the suitcase will start to take over those regions. That's what cortical remapping means—it's when brain functions and sensations start to become associated with neighboring brain structures meant for other functions and sensations.

For instance, in some trials involving people with amputated hands, when their faces were stroked they reported experiencing a sensation in their fingers. That's because the sensory inputs for the face are extremely close to those of the hand—which isn't physically there. Some of the sensory signals received by the part of the brain that controls the face spilled over into the part that would normally control the hand. The brain saw a brain structure that was still viable yet had no one telling it what to do—and thus it allocated it to a new function. The still-existing function simply took over the vacant lot and increased its bandwidth.

The phantom limb phenomenon may have dubious real-world usefulness, but it is a very real application of the brain trying to adapt, compensate, and grow.

When traditional medication obviously had no cure for phantom pain, Ramachandran conducted experiments on amputees with a device he designed: a "mirror box." This was a box that had two holes on one side; in one hole an amputee would place his still-existing hand, and in the other hole he "put" their phantom limb. In the box space between the holes, Ramachandran placed a mirror. The amputee would see his existing limb in the mirror, producing the visual effect that he still had two functional limbs.

Ramachandran encouraged the amputee to make a fist with his existing hand. When the amputee did so, he'd see both of his hands—his real one and the one in the mirror—coiling into a fist. Then Ramachandran had him uncoil his hand. In effect this was "tricking" the brain into seeing both hands perform the physical actions. Again, these physical sensations were all in the mind.

One of Ramachandran's subjects continually used mirror box therapy for a week—after which he reported that he no longer had the phantom limb sensation. It was completely gone, and his brain didn't register it at all. Theoretically, this was because his brain was getting so many conflicting signals that it ultimately "decided" there was no arm there. So the phantom vanished. Perhaps this is another piece of evidence to confirm the effectiveness of the placebo effect and how our beliefs can often create the reality we live in.

While not all of Ramachandran's subjects reported this result, the success of this one case suggests that neuroplasticity—the brain's ability to mold, fix, and change itself—is a powerful thing. It can even *over-repair* and *overcompensate* to the point of being detrimental, as the phantom limb phenomenon shows.

A Primer on Brain Structure

To understand the nature of neuroplasticity and the brain's ability to remake itself, it is helpful to have the basic orientation on how the brain is constructed. Knowing the main players in the brain's growth will prove beneficial when trying to ingrain positive patterns and responses. We'll try to keep this part short and snappy.

The *cerebral cortex* is probably the most recognizable part of the brain, as we've seen the brain depicted in biology textbooks—the gray matter that physically resembles a thick sponge. The cerebral cortex is the processor of thought, reason, language, and general consciousness. It may help to assign a so-called avatar to each portion of the brain, and since this portion is focused on analytical thought, this is the *Albert Einstein* portion. It is further divided into four subcomponents called *lobes.*

- *Frontal.* The front part of the cerebral cortex processes reasoning, expression, and body movement. This is where the iron rod blew through Phineas Gage's brain.

- *Parietal.* The middle of the cerebral cortex processes sensory information like touch, pressure, and pain. This area has the somatosensory cortex, and this is where the phantom limb is related to.

- *Temporal.* The bottom part of the cerebral cortex handles the interpretation of sounds and language through the *primary auditory cortex* and also processes memories through the *hippocampus.*

- *Occipital.* The back of the brain covers visual information we receive through the eyes.

The *brain stem* connects to the center of the brain and conducts all the messages the brain delivers to the various parts of the body. This coordinates all our body reactions and functions—eye and body movement, sleeping, blood pressure control, and so forth—based on the information relayed by the cerebral cortex. Simply, it keeps us alive. As far as avatars go, you can think of this as a starving man whose sole focus is on fulfilling his basic human needs and sustaining himself.

Other parts of the brain include the *cerebellum,* located at the back of the skull and in charge of muscle coordination; even though by size it is only 10% of the brain, herein lie 50% of the neurons in the brain (avatar: fight scene choreographer), and the *basal ganglia*, a spiral-shaped group of nuclei connected to other brain parts and associated with eye movements, learning, motor skills, knowledge, and emotion (avatar: stunt man).

In considering neuroplasticity, a part of the brain that merits specific attention is the *limbic system*. This is a complex series of parts that conduct all matters involving emotions, stimulation, and memories. It's often the part of our brain that we want to shut off because it is behind most of our fears and anxieties. As such, we can think of an avatar for the limbic system as an easily spooked and skittish cat who runs from everything and everyone. Major components of the limbic system include the following:

- *Thalamus.* A mass of gray matter resting between the two halves of the brain, the thalamus relays sensory and motor signals, which help regulate the body's circadian rhythms and functions like sleep.

- *Hypothalamus.* Positioned directly below the thalamus, the hypothalamus controls responses to hunger and thirst, emotions, body temperature, and the automatic nervous system.

- *Amygdala.* A tiny oval inside each of the brain's hemispheres, the amygdala is the hothouse for emotions, survival instincts, memories, and sex drive.

Also part of the limbic system is the *hippocampus*, a prawn-shaped ridge on the base of each of the brain's lateral ventricles (basically the brain's fuel stations). The hippocampus's main objective is believed to be the formation and long-term maintenance of memories. As such, a useful avatar would be the elephant, known for its memory abilities. Out of all the parts of the limbic system, the hippocampus is the most relevant to neuroplasticity, which we'll get to in a minute.

Activity between all these parts of the brain occurs through *neurons*, the elemental nerve cells that run the whole show. Neurons transmit information to and from each other in the forms of both chemical and electrical stimulation. Different neurons relate to different parts of the body. While neurons can be of varying size, they all have a few common components:

- *Dendrites.* Tree-like structures that receive and transmit brain information.

- *Cell body* or *soma.* The "energy" source of neurons where signals are gathered and distributed.

- *Axons.* A fiber connected to the cell body that transmits the neural signal.

In a standard neural reaction, the dendrites receive information from the sensory receptors in the brain. They pass this information through the cell body, which delivers it to the axon. The resultant electrical impulse—which at this stage is known as "action potential"—travels the length of the axon until it reaches a gap between neurons called the *synapse.* At that point the signal either travels to the adjoining neuron automatically or gets a boost from helpful *neurotransmitters* (such as dopamine, serotonin, epinephrine, endorphins, and many others) that the axons release to help the signal crossover.

Neurons are unusual in that they don't reproduce themselves like other nerve cells. Once they're gone, they rarely get replaced.

But the brain *can* generate new neural *pathways* that can facilitate change in the communication between neurons. Generation of those new connections is right at the heart of neuroplasticity. Just imagine that a habit is nothing but a series of strengthened neural connections and pathways and you'll better understand the changes we want to create.

Next, we'll focus on the primary brain structures responsible for the change you seek to implement.

Brain Structures in Neuroplasticity

For our purposes of reshaping the brain and molding it to effect change, let's take a deeper dive into the specific brain parts and functions that are most deeply involved in neuroplasticity. We'll be coming back to these areas from time to time throughout the rest of this book. There are four main regions: the prefrontal cortex, the limbic system, the hippocampus, and the basal ganglia and striatum.

Prefrontal cortex AKA Albert Einstein. Everything starts in the prefrontal cortex, which is part of the frontal lobe. The prefrontal cortex is probably where most of us "exist" in our minds: the conscious and analytical part of us that makes choices based on the information we've obtained. It's basically the hub of "free will" and our personality development, including decision-making, planning, and thought and analysis. It's like the conference room of the mind.

The prefrontal cortex is where we try to organize our behavior and thoughts with the goals we've set up. It's typically associated with "executive function"— where we make judgments and decisions and formulate strategies to align our actions with our "beliefs," like moral or value judgments (good vs. bad, better vs. best), qualitative assessments (similarities and differences), consequential thinking (what will happen if certain actions are taken, what's the predicted outcome), and social behavior. We use the prefrontal cortex to predict stock market rises, strategize marriage proposals, figure out if we're going to dress up as a goth, and decide where to get lunch.

The prefrontal cortex, as you'll recall, is the part of poor Phineas Gage's brain that got shredded in his accident. It stands to reason, therefore, that his pre-accident personality reportedly vanished after his brain damage occurred: the social inhibitors that had kept him from being a lousy guy were permanently damaged.

If we're pondering the possibilities of neuroplasticity and neural change, the prefrontal cortex is where we begin and end. It must reflect your conscious and, eventually, subconscious thoughts. When we seek to create change, the prefrontal cortex is where it starts. We must consciously make a decision to engage in a course of action until neural connections are either made or strengthened, at which point they can become the type of behavior that other structures handle.

Unfortunately, it's clear that not all of our intentions translate into actions, and our tendency to act against our best interests is due to the next structure.

The limbic system AKA the skittish cat. Our prefrontal cortex is in a constant battle with the limbic system—the part of the brain that's unconsciously dictating our actions by focusing on fear, survival, needs, risks, and desires. The limbic system thinks it is still the year 10,000 BC and hasn't updated itself despite the world around it changing dramatically.

The limbic system is always watching out for us, which is great in theory, but it can also be unnecessarily restrictive. Imagine how phobias and anxiety can derail you despite your best intentions—those are both the result of the limbic system not being adequately balanced by the prefrontal cortex. Both the prefrontal cortex and the limbic system very badly want to make our decisions for us, and as such they're frequently battling each other for that responsibility. It's your good old-fashioned conflict between logic and emotion.

This struggle is what makes neural change and neuroplasticity so difficult. As your prefrontal cortex is making evidence- and logic-based decisions, your limbic system hijacks that process with its emotional response. When the limbic system overrides the reasoning abilities of the prefrontal cortex, it results in the formation of bad habits. It can be as simple as wanting to not bite your nails but biting them anyway when you feel stress. This results in neural connections that lead you down the path of additional nail-biting during stress instead of less.

The limbic system and the prefrontal cortex don't always butt heads. Occasionally the limbic system can spur emotional satisfaction that overlaps with the logical functions of the prefrontal cortex: solving a tricky math problem, finishing a crossword, getting a promotion, or resolving a dispute. But the limbic system is the very epitome of a double-edged sword: its pursuit of pleasure and/or relief can be so powerful that it will overwhelm the supreme reason of the prefrontal cortex, driving one to make unfortunate choices.

One function of the limbic system that can create chaos despite its best intentions is the *fight-or-flight* response. This subroutine happens whenever the brain encounters a frightening situation and is forced to decide whether to stay and confront the problem or get the heck out of Dodge and seek safety. The fight-or-flight response emerges from several different kinds of threats: an oncoming car (flight), a stovetop kitchen fire (fight, hopefully), a snarling attack dog (could go either way), or a vindictive father-in-law knocking at your door with a shotgun (you're on your own).

In a suddenly stressful situation, the body releases hormones that signal the body's sympathetic nervous system, which alerts the adrenal system to release hormones that spur the chemical production of adrenaline or noradrenaline. This causes the body to feel certain physical symptoms (high blood pressure, increased heart and breathing rates). The body doesn't return to "normal" until between 20 and 60 minutes after the threat goes away.

Obviously, the fight-or-flight response is key to one's ongoing survival—but it also has certain drawbacks. Most troublesome is the fact that it doesn't differentiate between *actual* threats or just *perceived* ones. Yes, it reacts to a speeding car going through an intersection and heading straight toward you. But it also reacts to misinformation that perpetuates fear of unrealistic events: the recurrence of diseases that have been cured, a swarm of killer bees, a zombie apocalypse, or a piano falling from a tall building. These just don't happen, not even the zombie apocalypse. And the limbic system's inaccuracy about such potential events is what leads to the development of phobias, which have an oversized influence on the super-reasonable prefrontal cortex.

Additionally, the amygdala, that tiny part of the limbic system, also causes some headaches for the prefrontal cortex. Similar to the fight-or-flight mechanism that calls up our survival instinct, the amygdala processes our emotional responses to outside stimulation. Working from information sent from the thalamus through the neocortex, the amygdala decides what emotion to feel and floods the brain with hormones.

This is all fine and well unless the amygdala processes the stimuli as a *threat*, in which case the thalamus bypasses the filtering neocortex altogether and sends info straight to the amygdala. *That* causes the amygdala to become a fight-or-flight arbiter on the spot, which usually leads to emotion-driven decisions—which can be very bad (though not always). The amygdala encourages a response that's more reactive than thought-out. This is when we lash out at a friend or loved one for being five minutes tardy or physically lunge at someone who insults our mother.

As you can see, neuroplasticity in the way we want is not always easy when it feels like we can't even dictate our behavior on a daily basis. But that feeling in itself is the result of neuroplasticity! It's only when we can override existing neural connections resulting from overactive limbic systems that we can move forward.

Other components of the brain involved in neuroplasticity deal with the formation of learning, memories, and habits. By their very nature, these structures are involved in neural change.

Hippocampus AKA the elephant. As the center of learning and memory in the brain, the hippocampus is a prime target for neural change and neuroplasticity. The hippocampus deals with memory processing—especially during sleep—by consolidating and contextualizing memories we make every day. The hippocampus is *not* where we "store" memories; instead, it manages them and sends them off to various places in the cortex for long-term storage. Think of it as the relay station.

The hippocampus is extremely responsive to neural changes—especially, unfortunately, when it gets damaged. People who suffer injuries to the hippocampus often develop amnesia or extreme difficulty in remembering events, names, and dates. As a person ages, their hippocampus typically shrinks by around

13%, which is a substantial amount. Reduction of the hippocampus can also lead to Alzheimer's disease.

But the hippocampus also reacts to positive efforts to change its composition, or neuroplasticity. About 700 new brain cells generate every day in the hippocampus, one of the few areas where neurogenesis exists, so it's constantly changing on its own. Physical exercise is one of the best ways to enlarge the hippocampus, and damage can even be repaired by taking antidepressants, eating foods high in Omega-3 fatty acids, and abstaining from alcohol. One can even improve the hippocampus by taking on a new language or challenging themselves to solve problems or learn a new and complicated subject.

Basal ganglia and striatum AKA the choreographer and stunt man. Neural change is also prevalent in the basal ganglia, which is highly associated with habits and behavior. It's vital in the process of learning new habits through neural activity that occurs in the striatum, a part of the basal ganglia that focus on movement, among other things.

Neurons in the striatum act in very specific ways when a creature is learning (or acquiring) a certain habit. When an animal's just starting to learn a new routine, the neurons in the striatum fire constantly. As the animal develops and performs the habit over again, the neurons in the striatum fire only at the beginning and at the end of the activity. The striatum "groups" or "chunks" a series of activities as a single thing that only fires off when the whole sequence starts or ends—it's been etched into the neural pathways. That's how habits develop, for better or worse.

All of these parts of the limbic system are constantly butting up against the rational prefrontal cortex, causing illogical reactions that can make one feel out of control. But through effective neuroplasticity, those parts can be retrained and remodeled—and the results can literally be life-changing.

The Triune Brain Theory

If you're still having a hard time understanding how the brain is constantly battling itself and making neuroplasticity something you have to proactively strive for, a hypothesis exists that might serve as a helpful representation. It's called the *triune brain theory*, and it was developed in the 1960s by neuroscientist Paul D. MacLean.

To be forthright, it's not something we can accept as biological fact—in fact, most scientists today don't subscribe to it. But it could help to visualize the process of understanding the concept of the wars the brain puts itself through. It's also a great way to explain what you're up against when you're trying to effect neuroplasticity.

Roughly put, the triune brain theory assigns every human three brains (congratulations). Two of them are the brain regions we've already discussed: the prefrontal cortex and the limbic system. We know they are in constant battle with each other, which prevents neuroplasticity. The third one roughly corresponds to the basal ganglia, the habit-processing part of the limbic system we just described.

The first "brain" was described by MacLean as the *neomammalian complex*—what we've described as the prefrontal cortex. This is the kind of structure that's exclusive to so-called "higher" mammals, like human beings and other very closely related primates. It gives us our capacity for thought and consciousness, language, planning, and so forth. Unfortunately, this is not where our priorities lie.

The second "brain" is the *paleomammalian complex*, or what we've discussed as the overall limbic system. As the name implies, MacLean likened this part of the brain to older, prehistoric mammals who didn't have much immediate need for reflection or deep understanding—they just needed to feed themselves, procreate, and watch after the kids. But they needed to have a sensation that spurred these activities on: to eat, they needed to feel hungry. So the paleomammalian complex reflects those primal urges: hunger, sexual arousal, parental drive, and the emotions they call up. This is where our priorities lie, first and foremost. Thus, it is *away* from here that we want to rewire our neural pathways.

The third "brain" is the *R-complex*, or the *reptilian complex*. This loosely corresponds with the basal ganglia. It's so named because scientists used to believe that reptiles (and birds, for that matter) were driven by raw instinct more than carefully considered need and biological imperative. We're talking domination and aggressive attacks on other species, territorial marking, and ceremonial acts (like a peacock showing its plumage). We also want to rewire our neural pathways away from this brain.

The triune brain theory simply states that these three "brains" are always at each other's, well, throats. Your rational, advanced human brain knows full well that it needs to do certain very practical things and that if you do them fully, you'll more likely get positive results. But the caveman-like paleomammalian brain is always interrupting the prefrontal cortex with its primitive urges and emotions. And when you throw the reptile brain on top, with its raw hunger and savagery, forget it—all your best-laid plans are now in utter chaos. The change you want requires your neomammalian brain to constantly win, but that's tough to accomplish. It's a literal battle to carve out the neural change you desire.

Another way to think about the arrangement of the brains is in terms of energy expenditure. The prefrontal cortex needs a lot of gas to do its work. You have to constantly call up the reserves to think thoroughly about a situation, ponder the pros and cons, create something, predict an outcome—it's literally brainpower, and you need it to think things through. The limbic system, on the other hand, is almost automatic. It takes nothing to process emotions or instantaneously react out of mere instinct. The limbic system loves the path of least resistance because it's easier and takes less energy to maintain. The reptilian complex falls somewhere in between.

Once again, the introduction of the triune brain is for illustrative purposes only. It's a fair model to explain what areas are most responsive to (and maybe most in need of) neuroplasticity. It shows the constant conflict we face and why building a better brain is not as simple as making the decision to do so. It shows us why our actions don't match our intentions and how our brains work against us in many cases.

MacLean's triune brain shows the general overlay of neuroplasticity and the massive effort that must be undertaken. You *could* let yourself be taken in by your survival instincts, which lead to bad habits and destructive patterns of thought. This is where you would listen solely to your limbic system (paleomammalian brain and reptilian complex). It's usually the path of least resistance and the path of most immediate gratification. It's what most of us do day to day.

But neuroplasticity and the neural change you want is completely within your control. It's a lot more effort, and it requires delaying gratification, but the payoff can be immense. We can direct neuroplasticity ourselves to effect positive changes and habits in our lives. And this book will explain how.

Takeaways:

- What does it mean to build a better brain? Are our intelligence, functioning, and behaviors a result of our brains? In a nutshell, yes. Our brains are the center of who we are, and they dictate what we do even when we try to avoid it. Neuroplasticity is the process of the brain developing, changing, growing, and adapting to whatever it is exposed to, and it can be used to quite literally build a better brain.

- A couple of examples are stark illustrations of just how the brain can change, for better or for worse. Phineas Gage is a man who had an iron rod blown through a part of his brain. He lived and could still function as a relatively normal human being, albeit off-putting and fairly unpopular. This is because the iron rod tore through his prefrontal cortex, the portion of the brain responsible for personality and inhibition. This shows how the brain has separate structures for separate functions.

- Next, the phenomenon of phantom limbs is when amputees feel sensation or pain where their limbs used to be. This occurs because of cortical remapping, which is when adjacent parts of the brain take over parts that used to be used for the missing limb. This shows just how the brain compensates, heals itself, and changes physically.

- When it comes to specific brain structures, there are a few that we will focus on, as they relate to neuroplasticity and making changes. These include the prefrontal cortex, which is where conscious and analytical thought occurs; the limbic system, which is the emotional system that clashes with the prefrontal cortex; the hippocampus, where memory is processed; and the basal ganglia, where habits are formed and processed. Neuroplasticity is neutral, occurs in response to what it sees, and can be beneficial or detrimental.

- A helpful framework for understanding how neuroplasticity works is the triune brain theory. While not 100% correct and precise, it makes clear the forces at play in making neural changes. This theory states that there are three primary brains that are always at battle: the neomammalian (roughly corresponding to the prefrontal cortex), paleomammalian (roughly corresponding to the limbic system), and reptilian brain (roughly corresponding to the basal ganglia). The latter two brains are instinctual and subconscious, while changes made have to be conscious and thoughtful at first, so neuroplasticity depends on the ability of the neomammalian brain (prefrontal cortex) to win a certain percentage of the time.

Chapter 2. Plasticity in All Forms: How Does the Brain Change?

In 1970 two scientists from Cambridge University ran an unpleasant and borderline cruel experiment on kittens.

For five months, Colin Blakemore and Grahame Cooper raised kittens in closed-off environments where they could only see horizontal or vertical lines. They were placed in cylindrical containers with either horizontal or vertical lines on the walls, never both. When caretakers took them out to feed or handle the kittens, they wore clothing that was covered in either horizontal or vertical lines. For all intents and purposes, these two groups of kittens experienced different versions of reality. After being shut into those environments for five months, researchers took them out to see how they'd fare in a world with both horizontal *and* vertical orientation.

Would their eyes have adapted to their version of reality? Was there going to be any difference at all?

The kittens, it turned out, couldn't recognize objects or patterns of the kind that they weren't exposed to in their sealed-off environment. The kittens raised in the horizontal chambers could not see vertically-aligned objects; they kept bumping into chair legs and weren't responsive when researchers thrust a finger toward them in a vertical direction. Meanwhile, the vertical cats couldn't find an appropriate place to lie down and take a nap, since they had no ability to recognize horizontal planes. This surely resulted in some YouTube-worthy videos of kittens being clumsy.

Some of the kittens in the experiment successfully rehabilitated in a few weeks, but many never did. Their primary visual cortexes had been engineered so strongly in one angle that they were effectively blind to whatever lines they weren't exposed to during those five months. This is an example of neuroplasticity that affects the very perception of reality.

Then there is the case of taxi drivers and bus drivers in London. Researchers from the University of London studied and compared their brain structures in 2000 and discovered something notable: the taxi drivers had measurably larger hippocampi than the bus drivers. Why might this be? The theory behind their findings was that taxi drivers had to essentially memorize the entire road map of London—they needed to know the best shortcuts and alternate courses to take, and that required in-depth knowledge about every street and alley in town. It's something that could take months or even years.

The bus drivers, on the other hand, only had to drive a couple of pre-planned routes every day with little or no variation. They only needed to memorize a few turns and perhaps not even the street names. They could do it through visual memory alone, recognizing buildings or landmarks. However many people are on the bus makes no difference to the bus driver, as they already know the path and endpoint. However, being a taxi driver is somewhat like playing Russian Roulette—you never know what you're going to get or how to get there. (Okay, maybe that's more Forrest Gump than Russian Roulette.)

Recall that the hippocampus is directly linked to memory-processing—clearly the taxi drivers memorized more and interacted with their memories more on a daily basis, and thus the hippocampi were larger. Now, here is an example of neuroplasticity that gets us closer to what we're looking for.

But don't forget about the Moken children. They're a nomadic tribe who occupy a group of tropical islands in Thailand. These "sea gypsies" spend the large majority of their lives on boats in the middle of the sea.

They also have the uncanny ability to see extremely well underwater, even at substantial depths—handy when they need to catch fish on a daily basis. The Moken can do this because they've taught themselves how to regulate the shapes of the lenses and pupils of their eyes, as dolphins and seals do. They were able to constrict those individual eye parts by as much as 22% when underwater.

One might think that trait is just part of the genetic code of the Moken, who have developed it just as Charles Darwin's finches developed different characteristics as a result of adaptation to different environments. But that's because we assume our pupils and lenses just adjust themselves and that it's an innate act that we can't control.

This would be proven wrong. A Swedish researcher tried to train a group of European children how to manipulate their eyes the way the Moken did—and after just 11 sessions in one month, they were able to see underwater just as well as the Moken. This is an instance of neuroplasticity, as it relates to developing the ability to control your body and kinesthetics.

While we're at it, let's talk about musicians. Researchers found that the brains of professional musicians have a higher volume of gray matter in portions of their brains responsible for auditory processing and motor functions and of course related to musical abilities. Amateur musicians had slightly less gray matter, and non-musicians had least of all. For neurological purposes, the greater the amount of gray matter in a certain area, the more developed and robust the underlying ability is. Just like with the London taxi drivers, repetitive usage and exposure caused specific neuroplasticity.

However, such neuroplasticity is a double-edged sword for musicians. Among musicians who used two fingers simultaneously to play an instrument (such as a rock bassist), their brains had mapped those two fingers together so that the musician couldn't move one without moving the other, a phenomenon called *focal dystonia*. Remember the homunculus?

Imagine that its two fingers merged into one larger section. Their brains adapted in such a way that they had to undo that condition through specialized training to play other instruments effectively. This certainly brings new meaning to why budding musicians are always chided to "practice perfect" or "practice slowly"— because the practice will become embedded in the brain, for better or worse.

Then there are the Russians and linguistic relativity. A long-standing theory called the *Sapir-Whorf hypothesis* maintains that our patterns and systems of thought derive heavily from the language we use. One example of this theory in action is how Russian language speakers define colors in comparison to other tongues. Whereas Westerners might refer to different shades of blue as "light" and "dark" blue, Russians have two completely different words to distinguish between the two: *siniy* and *goluboy*.

That makes Russians slightly faster in discerning the two colors—which they perceive as having completely different names—than other dialects that only see them as alternate shades of the same color. This demonstrates neuroplasticity as a consequence of simple linguistic changes.

Finally, there's the elderly. The common belief is that the brain deteriorates as people age. But recent research indicates that's not necessarily the case. In fact, it's been found that the brain never ceases making new learning cells and readjusting its neural connections. Previously, it was believed that the brains of children and young adults conducted neuroplasticity more regularly and that the process slowed down considerably as people got older. However, researchers found that old people's brains are just as malleable as those of younger folks—just in a different way. Old people's brains develop new "circuits" and different connections to their frontal lobes, which in turn open up new understandings and perceptions that only the rare young adult can develop. There is, it turns out, a biological basis for the notion of older people being wiser.

What do all these examples prove?

Neuroplasticity isn't just an unmanageable, innate consequence of what you're exposed to. It can be intentionally shaped through several factors like the environment, repeated activities, and linguistics. And it can, therefore, be trained.

You may not want to possess a map of London in your head, but you can use the same process to learn faster, develop better habits, grow self-discipline, and simply accomplish what you put your mind to. Neuroplasticity is the vehicle that allows those things. It simply allows you to translate intention directly to action instead of hoping for the best.

What Is Neuroplasticity?

The above accounts show that neuroplasticity is no joke. It may have sounded abstract or intangible from the prior chapter, but you can see that there are very real consequences, both negative and positive, from the brain's tendency to change. Neuroplasticity is how our brain adapts in ways that reflect our experiences and actions, though not necessarily our intentions. And we can channel this to improve our lives.

But first, we should distinguish between the two types of neuroplasticity: *structural* and *functional.*

Structural neuroplasticity concerns the neuronal connections of the brain and the strength of the neural network. Structural neuroplasticity takes place by literally changing the brain's structure to increase the efficacy of a particular set of functions or actions. It involves building or strengthening the synaptic connections between neurons that you need or want the most and scaling back or removing the ones you don't. Our neural networks change according to how regularly we employ them—if we don't require certain neural pathways in our regular lives, they're not going to stick around.

In plain English, we create neuroplasticity through repetitive actions and thoughts that eventually become habits, and in doing so we reinforce and improve the function of these neural pathways. Repeated behaviors create new patterns of thought and habits—little by little, neuroplasticity occurs and starts to wear a groove like a Zen garden or sandbox that gets raked repeatedly so that the grooves become deeper and deeper over time until they are finally unconscious and instinctual. The brain is always ready to begin this process, because ultimately, these grooves save the brain energy and allow it to do what it wants—habituate and conserve energy.

The London taxi drivers are an illustrative example of how structural neuroplasticity works. They've spent years cultivating intricate knowledge of the entire grid of London streets. The grooves have been worn deeply. The more they've practiced that mental training, the more automatic and quickly their decisions about routes and shortcuts become. The neural connections regarding directions and locations are incredibly strong and resilient, and it becomes easy to jump from one thought to the next.

It's not just because they have quick reflexes or physical stamina: it's because their brains have been conditioned through experience and practice over a long and hopefully profitable period of time. When one thought is sparked, the associated *generalized* thoughts that come after it fire more quickly and reliably the more we train it. Think of it as the taxi driver being able to recall one street and then suddenly being able to summon a mental picture of the entire neighborhood.

Structural neuroplasticity is really what underlies most of the changes we see and the ones we want. If you want to break a bad habit of smoking, it requires repetition of the behavior you want (not smoking, or rather satisfying your urges in another way, such as chewing gum) so *that* particular groove becomes worn and the action of not smoking becomes easy and natural.

Learning is nothing but creating and strengthening connections between independent pieces of information. Overcoming fears requires consciously digging the groove of courage and acknowledging that you will be fine no matter what happens. Discipline is about creating the groove of delayed gratification and comfort with discomfort. Accordingly, structural neuroplasticity is what this book focuses on.

If you have a thought, it causes a neural change. If you keep having the same thought, it becomes a positive feedback loop that reinforces and cements the change. In this way, your past does not determine your future. What determines it is only what you think in this very moment, and what you think in the future. All of your thoughts, actions, and behaviors are being recorded somewhere, and every day we have the choice of how we want to program our brains.

Functional neuroplasticity is much less common, as it involves the brain's ability to improve or retain functionality in cases such as when the brain is damaged. This involves more dramatic change of the cortical remapping variety.

Consider the amputees with phantom limbs we discussed in Chapter 1. Their neural pathways were creating sensations that didn't correspond to anything in the real world; they still felt the presence of something that wasn't there. That's because an area of the brain was starting to take over another area's functioning.

Remember that the homunculus is a shining example of how functional neuroplasticity works. Studies showed that parts of the brain that regulate the face are perilously close to the parts that affect the hand—over time, for amputees, the functionality of those unused brain structures was slowly subsumed by its neighbors. So while a natural curiosity, functional neuroplasticity is not likely something we can create without extreme sensory deprivation or unfortunate circumstances.

The Process of Neuroplasticity

The etymology of neuroplasticity is simple: the prefix *neuro-* refers to nerves or nerve cells, and *plasticity* refers to a certain object's capability of being molded or changed. Dr. Michael Merzenich defined neuroplasticity as "the brain's ability to change its anatomical, neurochemical, and functional performance status across the lifespan."

Any given person's brain is different because their neuroplasticity has been entirely unique. Your thoughts, activities, behaviors, beliefs, and experiences all have direct impact on the shaping of your brain. Because nobody besides you has ever been through what you've been through, that means your brain's been molded by a completely singular series of patterns nobody else can ever quite duplicate— which means, in turn, that your brain is the only one of its kind.

Neuroplasticity happens from the moment one is born. A newborn baby's brain is a total blank slate, entirely uninformed. But it's structured to start taking input right away—its cerebral cortex is ready to build its complex neural pathways. The first few years of a child's life are the time when its brain development is the fastest, but not necessarily because the young brain is more malleable. Information is being constantly created and analyzed and it's coming in fast. Again, this is primarily structural neuroplasticity in creating synaptic connections and strengthening existing ones.

As the child grows into an adolescent, some parts of the massive influx in the brain that's happened to them become unnecessary to retain. That's when the brain starts going through something called *synaptic pruning*: it gets rid of the synapses that we haven't been using and keeps the ones that we have used most often. By the time a child reaches the age of 10, he or she has already dumped half of all the synapses they had at the age of two. (This is why we rarely remember anything from the first two years of our lives.)

When we become adults, our brain development cools off from the rapid-fire pace it experienced as kids. As we advance in age, we do lose brain cells and certain neural connections in the interest of efficiency and laziness. We begin to lose brain cells at a higher rate than we form new ones, and this is what causes many elderly people to suffer mental decline. However, what we *don't* lose as we get older is the brain's ability to rewire itself. We might drop a couple of brain cells (well, more than just a couple), but we never lose the ability to alter and strengthen our neural pathways. We *can* change how our synapses fire and the connections that we build.

Learning and having new experiences are the primary ways we restructure our neural pathways. Taking on new skills or knowledge directly affects the function and organization of our synapses, and that can happen at any time. It's something we actually *can* control.

And we actually *should*, because neuroplasticity doesn't always have a positive result. Brainpower is a lot like muscle power in that if you don't use it, you lose it. If one doesn't use a certain neural connection regularly, it dies off. Certain parts of the brain even decrease in size if they're not regularly employed. That's not terrible in and of itself—a concert pianist isn't going to use all the same brain functions that a lumberjack does, so they're just not going to *need* them. But on the other hand, by not developing and thereby losing synaptic exchanges, we could be limiting our own potential.

There are also certain neural connections that aren't positive at all. Bad physical habits, substance abuse or addiction, and negative self-talk can also become encoded and entrenched in neural pathways. The brain's reward system doesn't always distinguish between helpful pleasures and harmful ones. The hippocampus remembers and encodes the pleasure one might get from the taste of cheese puffs, driving 100 miles an hour, or the high of a drug just the same as it processes the happiness of getting a diploma or falling in love. All the amygdala knows is that it feels great and it develops a conditioned response—its neural pathways are set, and not for the best.

Scientists have also found a difference between the neural pathways of domesticated and wild animals—namely, that domestication can have adverse effects on neuroplasticity. The more civilized a being becomes, the smaller their brain gets.

For example, a domesticated dog has a smaller brain than its relative, a wild coyote. Anthropologists have discovered this disparity in the process of human history, as well.

Believe it or not, the brains of humans from 10,000–20,000 years ago were physically bigger than the ones we have now. That's the type of neural engagement that comes with a constant hunt for food and shelter and rarely having a moment for leisure or relaxation. Contrast that to today's preferred leisure activities, most of which include sitting still for extended periods of time.

Although it's a bit late for us to do anything about *that*, it does lend some credence to the idea that taking occasional chances and chasing unfamiliar experiences is more mentally beneficial than staying within our safe, comfortable, unchallenging existences. The less challenge and unfamiliarity, the less our brains have to work and adapt, and this is a negative consequence of our easier, modern lifestyles. Inducing the neuroplasticity we want is inherently tough and uncomfortable, precisely because it involves unfamiliarity and wearing a new groove where none existed before.

It's inevitable that our brains will change and develop throughout our lives. But again, it's something we can control. It forces us to become a lifelong learner. The more we engage and expose our brains to new challenges, the more we actually, physically reshape the structure of our neuronal networks. Studies have shown, for example, that taking art lessons have a direct impact on our fluid intelligence, attention span, and even overall IQ. Making music has been linked to better memory, increased learning ability, and greater attention span as well.

We'll talk more about this notion in the following chapter on guiding principles for beneficial neuroplasticity. What's more, these positive effects happen in both children *and* adults—further proof that neuroplasticity can happen at any time and any age.

The Debate of Neuroplasticity

Scientists didn't always agree that the brain was capable of changing itself. Up until fairly recently, the general belief was that the brain only grew in infancy and childhood and that by the time one hits early adulthood the brain is done growing and its structure was set in stone. Researchers believed that neurogenesis— the formation of new neurons—ended shortly after birth.

This belief persisted in ancient times because the brain was considered fairly fixed and was believed to decrease in pure ability the older one got. Later minds believed that the inability of certain brains to recover from damage proved it was essentially finite. In that context, they weren't able to observe how the brain functioned or behaved on a microscopic level (which of course changed once advanced technology became available), and thus they had no reason to think differently.

But even during those pre-modern times, there were outliers who thought there was more to brain function that wasn't quite being picked up. In 1980, psychologist William James wrote in his book *The Principles of Psychology* that he observed "an extraordinary degree of plasticity" in organic matter—especially "nervous tissue," the fundamental building block of neurons.

Researcher Karl Lashley observed evidence of brain transformation in his study of rhesus monkeys. And just before brain science took a great leap forward in the 1960s, doctors noticed that certain older stroke victims could regain at least a little of their brain functionality. He might not have pictured it to be as complex as the cortical remapping we've discussed, but this spurred him to suppose that neuroplasticity, or some form of neural regeneration, was possible.

It wasn't until Dr. Michael Merzenich ran experiments in the early '70s that we obtained confirmation that the brain can change itself. Ironically, the goal of Merzenich's project was to prove the *opposite*—that the brain, for all intents and purposes, is set in stone, and once a part of it is damaged, what it once knew can't be relearned. Instead, Merzenich discovered that the entire brain is essentially one fluid learning organ that functioned as a whole: that if a skill is lost through damage to a particular part of the brain, *other* parts can potentially learn it as well.

This gets us back to the homunculus, the "little man" that best describes the process of cortical remapping. Merzenich found that if, say, the cortical map of the "hand" was blocked from sensory input and therefore inoperative, it could be reanimated through the stimulation of *other* cortical maps close to the hand on the homunculus—for example, the forearm or even the eye. It was a clear indication that the brain was capable of adapting in ways that were real and tangible.

Primary Aspects of Neuroplasticity

Merzenich's "discovery" of neuroplasticity obviously merited more research into the topic. It was a monumental discovery that could help answer questions not only about recovery and health care but in peak mental performance and boosting the brain power that we are born with. In the years since his findings on neuroplasticity, the scientific community has made more determinations about the process that furthered our understanding of it.

Brain plasticity varies according to age. Although neuroplasticity is a lifelong process, younger brains are more apt to grow and develop systems of organization. Therefore, the brains of young ones are more sensitive and receptive to certain stimuli than those of older people. You've probably heard that it's nearly impossible to become fluent like a native in a language if you learn it as an adult. While not a hard rule, there is some scientific grounding for this claim.

It involves more than just neural processes. Nerve cells don't operate alone when it comes to neuroplasticity: they do have a support staff. In particular, glial cells help to support and insulate neurons. Vascular cells, which carry nutrients throughout the body, are also important in the process (and might explain why good nutrition is especially important in neuroplasticity, along with everything else). Everything about the structure changes.

Brain plasticity happens in one of two ways. The preferred manner, of course, is through learning, experience, and memory, all of which contribute to shaping and defining the neural passageways. But it can also happen through damage to the brain, such as when it suffers through a stroke. Even then, damage from a stroke *can* be repaired. As mentioned, this is the difference between structural and functional neuroplasticity.

Environment is important in brain plasticity. A primary conduit of neuroplasticity is what we experience, which naturally comes from our immediate surroundings and what we go through day to day. Genetics may play a role as well, but at this point we know that neuroplasticity is a direct result of what the brain is exposed to over a period of time. If you are in an environment that forces a certain set of actions, thoughts, behaviors, or habits, then you're left with no choice but to change and adapt. We'll talk more about this soon, as this is known as using an *enriched environment.*

That's pretty much what it sounds like: a set of surroundings that make up a supportive and thoughtful place for quality mental and physical stimulation. What comprises an enriched environment is obviously different for everyone, but it's shown to stimulate production of new brain cells, especially in the parts of the brain that regulate mood and memory. Whether it's a place where one can more effectively learn without too much anxiety or simply get some quality sleep to create and prune synaptic connections, there's a lot of truth to the notion that being in the right environment is key, even in neuroplasticity.

Brain plasticity isn't always good. As I mentioned earlier, certain kinds of neuroplasticity—those that arise from drug use, bad habits, and negative self-talk—isn't what we'd call the "good" kind. Phobias, anxiety, and fear are genetic and instinctual from years of evolution, but many are learned through repetition, just like the multiplication tables or the capitals of the countries of the world.

From Synaptic Pruning to Neurogenesis

We now understand that the brain doesn't become a stationary object after a certain point in life. Synaptic pruning doesn't just whittle our brains down to nothing after a while. The brain actually continues to manufacture new brain cells and new neural passageways. Thanks to extensive research in the area, we also now know that there are things we can do to stimulate increased production and improvement of brain cells, which we call *neurogenesis.*

The brain starts making new cells when we're still in the womb. The fetal brain eventually creates almost a trillion new neurons in the nine months between conception and birth. That number is eventually reduced through synaptic pruning to about 100 billion, which is about the number that we maintain for the rest of our lives. Pruning and modification, as we've discussed, comes through experience determining which neural pathways we use and which we don't.

Once we're born, the production of new brain cells slows down, and the production remains *definitely* in only two parts of the brain. One is the hippocampus, our main source of learning and memory. The other is the subventricular zone, which produces more neural cells than any other region in the brain for eventual distribution to the forebrain. Other studies have suggested, though not conclusively, that the subventricular zone also sends brain cells to the olfactory bulb (which handles our processing of new smells). But then again, the sense of smell is strongly related to memory, and it is common for smells to conjure up far-away and long-ago situations and people.

Almost any activity that engages the mind has been shown to stimulate the production of brain cells—including mental activities like psychotherapy, performing stimulating tasks, learning, and even just reflecting on our thoughts (especially the positive ones). But it can also be generated through physical activities like exercise. Additionally, certain medications have been shown to stimulate neurogenesis.

In both neural pathway generation and synaptic pruning (which actually doesn't stop until we're well into our 20s), our brain creates new connections through the growth of dendrites and axons, especially during sleep. The production of new pathways and the deletion of unused ones is informed by our personal experiences and what we think, do, or say.

Creation of new connections is impacted by almost anything that interacts with the brain: words, thoughts, memories, meditation, heightened attention, and especially new learning. The new cells that form in the hippocampus are especially linked to learning: they're much more likely to respond to brand new information than older neurons, are more moldable, and are more capable of learning and memorizing newly introduced, complicated concepts. The formation of new neural connections— especially important to consider, since we never stop making new ones even after brain cell production slows down—is particularly responsive to mindful activities.

There are several factors that work *against* neuroplasticity. Lack of sleep is one of the most damaging, and high levels of stress and gastrointestinal disorders have also been shown to have a negative impact. And despite the fact that our neural activity doesn't *stop* as we get older, the stimulation of new brain cells does decrease with age. That's really what causes seniors to degrade, not necessarily a high level of synaptic pruning. There is some level of control we can exert over those factors (except getting older), so monitoring them and their effects on our lives is a key step in directing our brain plasticity.

At this point, you understand the brain and just what it takes to effect change upon it. The neural growth you desire is within your grasp, as are the benefits that come with it. When you view your mental performance as a result of the number of neuronal connections you cultivate, or the greater number of dendrites you recruit on a daily basis, it suddenly becomes very clear how to build a better brain.

In the next chapter we'll examine some of the key principles of neuroplasticity in finer detail.

Takeaways:

- What is neuroplasticity? We've perhaps danced around it, but we get down to the details here. It is the changes in your brain that are neutral by themselves and simply a reflection of our actions, thoughts, habits, environments, and so on.

- There are two types: structural and functional. Structural neuroplasticity concerns strengthening and creating neural connections over time, while functional is what happens when specific parts of the brain lose functionality and are compensated for by neighboring brain elements. Phantom limb sufferers who unknowingly utilize cortical remapping are using functional neuroplasticity, while learning new habits and information comes through structural changes.

- We mainly seek structural neuroplasticity for obvious reasons. One study in particular illustrates what neuroplasticity is all about: scientists have determined that animals that have been domesticated have smaller brains, and they've found that this finding also applies to human beings. Thus, neuroplasticity's changes aren't always positive or beneficial. That's why we must be proactive and intentional—the more challenge, discomfort, and effort spent, the more neuroplasticity will occur and the higher functioning our brains will be.

- Neuroplasticity was first thought to be impossible and then thought to be reserved only for children. Both of these notions were eventually proven wrong over time. Though we still suffer synaptic pruning throughout our lives, neuroplasticity also occurs throughout our lives, and neurogenesis has even been found in select portions of the brain, specifically those related to smell and memory—which, coincidentally, have been found to be related to each other. The brain changes and adapts only to what it experiences, and this is within our control.

Chapter 3. Principles of Neural Growth

Ned always thought he was "slow." He didn't really have any proof to back this notion up, but his job at a local assembly plant didn't require him to use much in the way of brainpower. His grades in school were always mediocre, and he didn't enjoy reading.

Ned's uncle Jack—who was very friendly but frequently described by Ned's dad as "crazy"—died and left Ned his guitar. Ned had heard his uncle's stories about traveling across Europe, entertaining strangers with his music at cafés and bars. Jack remembered every town he'd visited and often told stories about the people he'd met on his trips. He seemed to have an inexhaustible well of local folklore and legends from all around the continent. Although his dad thought they were "nutty" stories, they always enraptured Ned when he was a kid.

Ned figured he'd pay tribute to his uncle by learning how to play the guitar. He actually assumed that's why his uncle left it to him in the first place. But learning it required a whole new skill set—actually, more like four or five skill sets. It wouldn't be easy. But he went ahead with it anyway. He ordered books that showed all the chord formations. He practiced rigorously and vigorously. He forced himself into a strict practice schedule of twice a day for 45 minutes each session. He never missed a day if he could help it. When his fingers hurt too much at first, he simply iced them and played for as long as they would remain numb, only to repeat the process again.

After about a year of self-training, Ned got up the nerve to play at a local open mic. It went better than he imagined; he started to feel that he wasn't so slow after all if he could learn the guitar himself and accomplish this.

Now, we don't know if Ned really is slow or not. But we do know that he took advantage of a few of the guiding principles of neural change and growth to get to his level of skill with the guitar. He found a personal interest, diligently worked at it, applied himself, and most definitely challenged himself at the end by performing.

In the end, he trained his brain and that's what is important. Suppose Ned was slow in other areas of life or academia—but it ultimately doesn't matter to the type of intelligence or mental performance that you want for yourself. It's just a matter of knowing what it takes.

In this chapter we'll be looking at four specific principles that will guide you in your quest for neural growth. What best practices will spur the creation and strengthening of neural and synaptic connections? What can you do to reinforce the pathways that you need to bring about the change you want? This chapter will lay the groundwork for you to build a better brain.

But before we start, let's be honest about one thing: this isn't going to be a cakewalk. The road to neuroplasticity is not a six-lane highway—it's more like a steep, crooked trail with twists, bends, and possibly a mountain lion. That's simply the nature of neural growth. You have to work more deliberately. It requires you to build those grooves in your brain, and you have to work even harder to reset a currently undesirable groove. You might consider it to be too difficult, taxing, and time-consuming. However, if it *were* easy, it wouldn't work. No neural groove is worn if you don't walk the path.

The one rule about bringing about neuroplasticity is that if you're sailing through it, nothing's really happening. Synaptic connections get created through challenge and exertion. For instance, for physical fitness, simple exercises like taking a 10-minute stroll in the park aren't very beneficial or effective in getting you closer to your goal (unless you are *truly* lacking in fitness, but that's another book entirely).

To that end, let's address those many online sites and mobile apps that promise to increase your neuroplasticity with so-called *brain-training* games. I'm sure you've seen them: the ones that say you can increase your mental strength or speed of thought with a daily series of fun-looking memory or cognitive games that look like Centipede or Pac-Man with flashcards. They promise to jack up your brainpower and skyrocket your IQ—all for a reasonable monthly subscription fee. Some of them pop up in the same manner as more lewd propositions, while others look legitimate, complete with pictures of people in white laboratory coats and glasses.

As you might suspect, these sites' claims aren't backed up by science. Their promises to increase your brain power are nothing more than marketing fodder. It's a sexy proposition—play a game for 20 minutes a day and become *smarter*—but if it sounds too good to be true, well, you know what follows.

In fact, one of the best-known companies in the space, Lumosity, outright said their programs will help brain plasticity and got hit with a $2 million fine by the Federal Trade Commission for false advertising. An independent review of 18 such online resources found that 11 of them used absolutely no scientific evidence to support their claims, and that's to say nothing about actual effectiveness in terms of intelligence or mental agility.

Like many things, people only need to hear something they desire in order for them to suspend disbelief or critical thinking. These brain-training companies were profitable because people can draw the conclusion that engaging the brain in general is good for performance, much like running is good for people's overall physical performance. But the brain is quite a bit pickier; it deals in *specificity*, which means that practicing math won't help you write a better essay; it will only help your math skills. We know this to be true when we understand that practicing the piano probably won't help with your chess skills. Additional studies found that participants engaging in brain games improve in their ability to play the games, but these skills did not transfer between different tasks, and their proficiency at specific games also added after pausing for a couple of months.

About the best I can say about such sites is that their games probably won't *hurt* your efforts toward neuroplasticity. They'll certainly help you improve at the particular task you are engaging in, such as remembering odd combinations or seeking novel patterns. However, that has nothing to do with thinking smarter, unless you are being tested on remembering odd combinations or seeing novel patterns in that exact context. They're not going to do all that much to help you with getting anything other than a minor sense of accomplishment.

The Stanford University Center on Longevity and the Berlin Max Planck Institute for Human Development had this to say about brain training games: "The strong consensus of this group is that the scientific literature does not support claims that the use of software-based "brain games" alters neural functioning in ways that improve general cognitive performance in everyday life, or prevent cognitive slowing and brain disease."

Again, if you want to get *real* work done, you're going to have to work a little harder and more deeply—but at least you won't have to pay a subscription fee to "unlock more levels."

With that out of the way, what *should* you do? Keep in mind the rule of thumb that if it's easy, it's not doing anything for you. Here are four principles that should underlie all your efforts toward neuroplasticity and the type of mental performance you want.

Principle #1: Stimulation Is Key

The driving force behind the workings of the brain is pure and simple *activity*. Remember the analogy of raking a Zen garden from earlier? The more raking, the deeper the grooves and the closer you are to your goal. Stimulation, action, activity, and motion—all in a repetitive manner—

are the backbone of neuroplasticity. It doesn't happen passively to any degree; it must be proactively sought out by you.

Neuroplasticity itself is nothing more than stimulation in a controlled and directed manner. The more stimulation, the more neural connections are built. The more connections, the quicker you think. The quicker you think, the more additional connections you can make between unrelated information and thoughts. Stimulation through brain training games is fairly useless, but consistently engaging your brain on a deeper level is something different.

You can think of essentially all learning as a type of stimulation. In fact, let's imagine that you want to learn a new language, Spanish. Learning a new vocabulary word once without mentioning it again is not so much stimulation, but the groove begins to wear deeper each time you review it. But remember, reviewing the vocabulary word incorrectly also wears a groove, so you have to be careful about your stimulation.

What kind of activity stimulates the brain the most? More than anything else, it's the kind of activity and learning in which one tackles unknown and foreign subjects, things with which one doesn't have a lot of familiarity. Learning a new language from scratch is especially good, as are learning a new musical instrument, cooking unfamiliar cuisines, or teaching yourself about subjects in science, math, or philosophy that are particularly challenging.

If you're wondering why everyone isn't keen to hop on the train of optimizing their brain's functioning, you can a common thread here: it requires the opposite of pleasurable activity. Think of stimulation as a workout for your brain. If you do the equivalent of jogging for only five minutes, you'll have negligible benefits. However, if you do the equivalent of running hard for an hour, that's where things start to change.

One helpful approach to increase stimulation is to employ "whole brain thinking," which entails engaging both hemispheres of the brain as much as possible. Though it's essentially a disproven myth in education about mental faculties and the two hemispheres having mutually exclusive functions, it can still be a useful roadmap to think about how to keep stimulated and keep active and in motion.

For instance, traditionally, the myth calls for the left hemisphere to be associated with logical and analytical pursuits, while the right hemisphere is associated with artistic, emotional, and creative endeavors. Activities that are most powerful for stimulated thinking engage left-brain functions like analysis, ordered sequencing, math and science skills, planning, and verbal expression. They also embrace right-brain strengths like intuition, interpretation, emotional thought, imagination, creativity, and nonverbal expression.

Learn to play chess but also attempt to paint occasionally. Read historical biographies but also seek out music by your favorite artists. Whatever you do, don't just watch television—unless it's a documentary!

Perhaps the way to understand this principle is that continuous lifelong learning is what keeps our brains the healthiest over our lifetimes. Researchers at the University of Texas in Dallas determined that, even at an advanced age, learning an unfamiliar skill can effect positive changes and improvements to the brain. For their study, they assigned 200 senior citizens the task of learning a new skill. Some were taught to quilt, and others were taught digital photography editing.

For three months, the subjects spent fifteen hours a week learning their new skills. After that period, they were administered memory tests, which were also taken by control groups of senior citizens who did other activities, like socializing or playing easy games at home, but didn't learn a new skill. The researchers also tested their memories a year after the first round of study was complete.

The results weren't even close: the older folks who learned new skills showed huge improvements in memory over those who didn't—both immediately after the first trial and a year later. The greatest improvement was seen in the subjects who learned Photoshop, because it was more difficult to learn than quilting. (Younger generations may dispute that, but many of the older subjects had little or no experience with computers, so there was quite a learning curve adjustment for them.)

This is the principle in stark action: learning new skills strengthens the connections between different parts of the brain. By tackling a completely unfamiliar challenge, even in short bursts over an extended period of time, the skill-learners were still able to create change on a physiological level. In fact, the greater the struggle and challenge (and assumedly the greater the amount of new information learned), the better the subjects performed on memory tests.

Anytime you make a proactive decision to take on a new skill and stick with it through the early, more difficult stages, you're going to improve your neuroplasticity and reap the benefits.

For example, if you're interested in cooking but don't know how, you probably won't get far if you stay in basic cheese sandwich mode. But you also don't want to start off with something that's hard to master, like consommé or a soufflé. Something that's feasible but still requires you to develop a technique might be the ticket, such as a respectable range of different pasta dishes and sauces.

Learn a variety of cooking techniques, commit some recipes to memory, and learn the basics of what types of tastes and textures go together. This alone will make you more formidable than the majority of home cooks, and you'll be forging new connections within your brain with each new recipe. Just remember to keep challenging and stimulating yourself with new recipes and techniques for optimal neural growth.

Learning a new skill has innumerable benefits, but it's not the only way to improve your thinking. There's also reading and consuming content in general, which

I'm trusting you're at least a little familiar with since you're doing it right now.

There's a lot of knowledge to be had out there. Being better informed is a sure way to improve your thinking and challenge your perceptions. Instead of learning a hobby, you are learning about new topics, fields, and disciplines. No matter the area, this is going to stimulate your brain and keep it engaged.

The goal with being informed is to expose yourself to as many sides of a topic or issue as you can. A comprehensive study of current events isn't complete without knowing the perspectives of as many varied people and views as you possibly can. What you dread the most, even a perspective, will create the most change and growth. Remember how the seniors who learned Photoshop performed the best on memory tests?

Imagine that strongly ingrained beliefs have created similarly strong mental pathways. You'll be creating completely new and novel neural pathways by challenging what's always been a given in your mind. More importantly, you'll gain the ability to step outside yourself and into someone else's viewpoint. Worst-case scenario, you *don't* change your mind.

There are a few more small ways to keep stimulated in daily life.

Go grocery shopping. As you add items to your cart, keep track of the total value of them in your mind. When you're just starting this practice, you can round up or down to the nearest dollar or half-dollar, but once you get going, you can *really* up the ante by figuring out the exact amount as you go. This builds up your brain's ability to make long computations of uncommon numbers.

When you meet a new person, memorize three different pieces of information about them *in addition* to their name—hair color, accent, where they grew up, what they do for a living, where they attended school, whatever. When you get home, enter all this information on an index card and file it in a box. From time to time, take out these cards and study them. This builds up your memory and attention to detail.

When you're at a special event that you want to commit to memory, try taking a few *mental* snapshots. Focus on a part of the event that you find emotionally or intellectually interesting and imprint the event in your mind. Yes, you can take a smartphone photo too—but that won't capture all the sub-visual details of the event or your sense of emotional placement. Taking a mental picture will help you increase your memory power in the future, beyond just your episodic recall.

Have a favorite popular song? Memorize the lyrics. You can find the lyrics to almost any recorded song by searching "[song title] lyrics" on Google. If it's a rap song with lots of words, all the better. (In fact, I strongly endorse a website that started as a hip hop-focused lyrics site, genius.com, which now has millions of pages for lyrics of all styles.)

Before you head off to sleep, think back on the events you experienced over the day that just passed. This is especially helpful in remembering small details and building your concentration—in addition to your skills of observation and interpretation.

Spend some time writing with your non-dominant hand. This can improve the integration between your brain's hemispheres, improve your creativity, and increase your open-mindedness.

Stop using a GPS in your car—use written directions and memorize maps. As you now know, your hippocampus will love you for it.

We touched upon synaptic pruning earlier, and it generally stands for the notion that if you don't use it, you lose it. Thus, it's also important to focus on pure mental stimulation because not using your brain in an active way will result in a gradual decrease in its abilities. This affects several crucial areas of functionality, especially memory, thought, attention, navigational skills, social actions, and other complex actions. And by the time you're 75, you've already lost 10% of the neurons you were born with—and even though the brain can replace them, it can't do so as fast as it loses them.

There are various reasons our brains just peter out. Our nutritional, cellular, vascular, and immune systems all play a part. But the biggest contributor is *disusing* the brain. This happens throughout our lives with synaptic pruning, but as we get older it *really* starts to play a part, as the neural pathways we don't engage start dropping out. For that reason, increasing meaningful stimulation is especially important as we grow older.

Principle #2: Enrich Your Environment

Surroundings play a large role in neuroplasticity. Really, our environment plays a large role in our entire lives, decisions, and sense of identity—though we might not always like to admit it.

While the first principle involves taking active steps to increase and cultivate neural connections, having what's called an *enriched environment* allows you to passively accomplish the same end result. It means setting up your environment so that building neural connections automatically happens whether you choose them to or not. Construct a stimulating environment that helps you to stimulate and engage your brain unconsciously—just because there's no other way for you to exist in that environment.

A quick illustration might be if your goal is to learn to swim and live on a small island for a period of time. It's not quite related to neuroplasticity, but it's an environment that leaves you with no choice but to engage in what you might avoid otherwise. Or if you wanted to learn a foreign language, you would change the language that your phone is set to, which would leave you no choice but to adapt!

The properly enriched environment can help stimulate neural growth even as we've aged beyond the heady times of childhood and young adulthood, when learning is at its most accelerated pace. Surroundings that provoke thought, seize your attention, and are full of novelty are ideal.

The importance of the enriched environment was first established in a study by Dr. Marian Diamond in the 1960s. Diamond placed rats in one of two different cages. One cage came complete with toys, balls, staircases, ramps, and wheels; the other just had the bare necessities of cheese and a water bottle. Diamond found that the rats in the "deprived" box suffered measurable brain atrophy, whereas the rats in the "stimulating" box did not. She made the first assertion that the enriched environment's ability to provide both physical activity and enjoyment through toys were important components of brain development (or at least the lack of brain atrophy).

Harry Harlow, a researcher best known for his extensive work with rhesus monkeys, conducted an experiment in which he placed the animals in a completely barren laboratory environment. This placement led some of the monkeys to develop behavioral flaws like "floating arm," in which the monkey suspended his arm in mid-air, apparently without knowing. When Harlow made improvements to the laboratory that made for a more stimulating environment, he noticed some improvement in the monkeys' behavior and fewer random flaws like floating arms. Here, there was again a link made between the environment and brain development.

Thankfully, scientific research in the matter of enriched environments was also performed with actual humans. Dr. Robin Green studied victims of traumatic brain injury and the long-term effects stimulating surroundings could have on recovery. Green's subjects had suffered their injuries five months before the trials and were studied for more than two years.

Green determined that patients who received higher stimulation in three social categories—physical, social, and cognitive—showed improvement over the course of the study. Subjects who were in situations where they could read, finish puzzles and problem-solving exercises, socialize, and complete some kind of physical activity showed less shrinking in their hippocampi than those who weren't. "After a serious brain injury, damaged tissue disconnects healthy areas of the brain," Green reported. "Those healthy areas are under-stimulated and, over time, deteriorate."

Enriched environments are really no different from tactics people employ to improve their habits or build self-discipline. If you're forced to do it, you'll do it—and conversely, out of sight, out of mind.

Enriched environments can contain elements that promote stimulation in a few specific categories.

Social. Quality interaction with the outside world is an extremely powerful agent of neural change, as it improves empathy, social intelligence, and sensitivity. This should be easy to understand in comparison with isolation, which can't be a very stimulating environment. How can you design your environment for this? By changing your environment to be more social and initiating more social activities. Become the planner in your friend group and make it a habit to engage with strangers.

Physical. A stimulating physical environment gives you the opportunity to respond to training and develop small motor skills and coordination. How can you design your environment for this? This could include anything from working at a stand-up desk, setting up a workout area in your garage (or sticking to your gym membership), or committing yourself to an hour of walking every day. Remember, the point of the enriched environment is to make your ideal outcome relatively unavoidable.

Sensory. There's more to having a nice houseplant than just making the room look good. An environment that engages the senses can open up worlds of experience that help in shaping your neural pathways and improve your awareness and overall sensory perception. This could take the form of having interesting music playing during waking hours, having a rotating series of interesting pictures on your TV screen (when not actively watching it), changing the pictures on your wall every few months, or keeping your house clean and pleasantly scented. For each of the five senses (vision, taste, smell, touch, hearing), you can consciously integrate them into your room, home, or work space.

Nutritional. The best environment will make it easy for you to stay healthy by improving your diet and physical fitness. In the enriched environment, this could mean keeping junk and artificial food out of your pantry, using spices to flavor dishes instead of salts and sugars, being open to cuisines other than your own heritage's, and water. Lots and lots of water.

Remember, the idea behind this principle is to force yourself to engage your brain. When you leave yourself no choice, you create faster neural change.

Principle #3: Be Methodical, Persistent, and Repetitive

Like any meaningful change, brain plasticity requires time, patience, and practice. It's not something that can be rushed through, and there is no quick and easy fix. A systematic and consistent approach is the best one to take when working on sharpening your brain. Even though we've used the Zen garden example frequently, for this principle, it is more illustrative to think about how the Grand Canyon was formed. At the bottom lies a small river, and through millions of years, this river slowly carved a chasm in the earth that is one of the biggest of its kind. That's an oversimplification of geography, but the idea that neuroplasticity is a long process should be clear.

Researchers Jeffrey Kleim and Theresa Jones came up with some guidelines for being methodical and persistent in neuroplasticity. They developed these guidelines in the context of helping victims of strokes and brain injury recover, but they can be appropriated for anyone trying to improve and strengthen their neural pathways. They generally found that the number one indicator of recovery was— you guessed it—consistency over time.

Habits aren't formed in a day (in fact, studies have shown it takes at least two months to form a habit) and it's near impossible to memorize all 50 states of the United States in one sitting. Your hair only grows millimeters a week, and your neurons don't forge connections instantaneously. Things take time.

Use it or lose it. As we've mentioned before in this book, neural pathways that are not being actively used instead get pruned. This is mainly a directive for you to keep at whatever efforts you're making and to engage as fully as you can to keep those pathways active. Pruning will inevitably happen, so it's important to focus on the functions and knowledge you want to develop to keep their respective pathways in the brain intact.

Repetition matters. Practice will pay off. When you find a course of action you want to focus on, be prepared to repeat it. Neural pathways respond to repeated practice by becoming more ingrained, and it gets easier as you go along. Just like "reps" in the gym do with your physical abilities, repeated exercises in building neural pathways will make your brain functions more automatic in time.

Intensity matters. Kleim and Jones also discovered that neural pathways respond more strongly to intense retraining. Although you may feel initially resistant to tasks that might seem a little too difficult or hard to grasp, those are exactly the kinds of efforts that will have the most effect on your synaptic connection. Sprinting is more beneficial than leisurely jogging. Learning a complex foreign language is one of the best ways to raise your mental level of intensity. If you've been intimidated by higher math studies like calculus, applied mathematics, or trigonometry, try teaching them to yourself from the ground up. That goes for any subject that tends to scare off people, be it art appreciation, law, complex science, or classical music theory.

Salience matters. Why you're embarking on efforts to improve neuroplasticity is just as important as how you go about them. If you're pursuing a line of activity that doesn't have any relevance to you or your life, it's not going to be as effective. If you're still deciding what to do, take some time to choose what kind of practice is going to mean the most to you. If you're in the middle of a course and discover it's not that critical to your needs, you may want to rethink and refocus your energies into one that is.

Transference and generalization matter. Learning a new skill is especially successful when you can apply what you're learning to multiple scenarios or functions. Something that's specific to only one or two subjects won't have any relevance in a more generalized way, though they may be extremely helpful in narrower fields. Try to employ at least a few "adaptable" areas of focus that will come in handy in multiple scenarios. The act of thinking how you can apply it in different contexts will also help. Learning a foreign language instills educational strategies that can help you with another language—if you learn French, you might be more able to learn Spanish at some point.

Principle #4: Take Care of The Engine

The brain is just like any other part of your body in that it needs to be taken care of physically. For neuroplasticity, that's doubly true. If your brain is deprived of nutrition and the proper amount of sleep, or if it's under the weight of stress, you won't have enough strength to effect neural change. Remember that neural change is an intentional, conscious effort, and the more challenging, the more effective it is. If you're simply too tired, dehydrated, or otherwise distracted, there is no chance of absorbing anything that would create change. You might be familiar with this—it's the feeling of reading the same page in a book multiple times and still not understanding or even really processing it.

Just like an athlete and her physical body, the brain must be ready for change and development, and the factors of stress, sleep, and exercise greatly influence that. For the most part, these elements are within your control, which makes them even more important. Let's begin our mini-tour of how neurological health is directly correlated to your brain's functioning and ability to institute neural change.

Stress is one of the biggest influences on the brain's health. If you want a clear and concrete illustration, you don't have to look any further than any veteran or trauma victim suffering from post-traumatic stress disorder (PTSD) and how their lives are negatively affected. They literally lack the ability to function in daily life because they are so tense and they are likely to snap at any given moment as an outlet for their anxiety and fear.

A plethora of research has found that stress impacts the brain's health and mental capacity in hugely negative ways. This is in large part due to the body's physiological response to stress. But first, it will be helpful to define the difference between the two main types of stress: chronic stress and acute stress.

Chronic stress is when you are under ongoing stress for a relatively long period of time—something as small as being under a constant heavy load at work or dealing with a relationship that is frequently combative. These are small sources of stress that seem insignificant until you look at the cumulative effects and realize that you are always on edge, testy, and tense with knots in your shoulders. When we are experiencing chronic stress (the amount of which is highly variable and relative to the person's tolerance), our body is in a state of physiological arousal. This is known as the fight-or-flight response, and it's our body's main defense mechanism when it senses a stressor.

It was once useful millennia ago when the terms "fight" and "flight" were truly taken literally—if the body sensed a stressor or a reason to be in fear, it would put itself on the highest levels of alertness and be prepared for a fight to the death, if necessary, or running away as quickly as possible. In either case, the body's hormones, heart rate, and blood pressure are highly elevated. The main stress hormone, cortisol, is released in spades and has been implicated in causing the alertness.

So if you are under chronic stress, you are permanently in this fight-or-flight mode of alertness and have spades of cortisol. Your body will very rarely reach the relaxation phase, which is known as a state of homeostasis. And unfortunately, cortisol impedes your mental abilities in lieu of risk analysis.

In other words, chronic stress makes you alert and physiologically aroused *all the time*. This is exhausting both physically and mentally and has the effect of shrinking your brain. Studies have shown that chronic stress has caused as big as a 14% decrease in hippocampal volume (the area of your brain responsible for memory encoding and storage), which is startling.

A study (Pasquali, 2006) showed that memory in rats was negatively affected when the rats were exposed to cats, which presumably caused stress. The rats that were exposed to cats far more routinely were unable to locate certain entrances and exits.

The difficult part is you may not realize you are under chronic stress, because it has become normalized for you. It is just like when your shoulders tense up—you probably don't realize it until someone points it out and you can see the contrast between being relaxed and being tense.

The cumulative effects of being constantly on edge, paranoid, unable to focus, and feeling despair and overwhelmed will catch up to you. Imagine being pumped up on adrenaline for days, weeks, or months. Not only will it impair your memory and brain processing, but it will leave you unable to function in general. Excess and consistent cortisol can cause a loss of neurons in the prefrontal cortex and hippocampus, as well as decrease the neurotransmitter serotonin, which is what creates the feeling of *happiness*. This is what people with PTSD suffer, but to a much higher degree.

Acute stress, on the other hand, is not something that will slide by unnoticed.

Acute stress is the sudden jolt of adrenaline you experience when someone cuts you off in traffic and you nearly crash or when you get into a heated argument. However, acute stress is momentary, temporary, and you can feel it and notice it. This is when adrenaline is coursing through your veins, leaving your palms sweaty and hands shaking. Your body is trying to give you the alertness and strength you need for anything. Intense bouts of acute stress can even cause headaches, muscle tension, upset stomachs, or vomiting.

If it persists and lasts for a longer period of time, it just may cross the threshold into chronic stress.

But the labels are unimportant. What's important is what happens to your brain's abilities when you are under any type of stress. Remember that neural changes are made with simple repetition over time. What happens when stress becomes the primary course of action?

Brain scans of stressed individuals showed less activity in the prefrontal cortex and more in the limbic system. Prolonged stress creates structural changes—the groove is being worn in such a way that you are creating a stressed brain unable to process in any other way.

The brain literally rewires to be more efficient in conducting information through the circuits that are most frequently activated. When stress is frequent, these pathways can become so strong that they become your brain's fast route to its lower, reactive control centers. Your primitive brain dominates more frequently, and you lose touch with your conscious, logical, and calm brain.

The next part of the healthy brain equation is sleep. It has long been argued that specific modes of sleep are where memories are actually created and where learning can be said to occur. It is thought that the brain's structure is changed and synaptic connections are formed during sleep.

Indeed, studies have teased out the specifics of how memories are enhanced or stored during sleep. In a 2005 study, Professor Matthew Walker of Harvard University was able to compare fMRI scans of the brains of subjects while awake and asleep to see the different parts of the brain that were activated—where memory consolidation occurred. He found that people's cerebellums were far more active after a period of sleep between periods of learning, and this activity was highly correlated with better learning and memory.

Professor Walker commented, "Sleep appears to play a key role in human development. At twelve months of age, infants are in an almost constant state of motor skill learning, coordinating their limbs and digits in a variety of routines. They have an immense amount of new material to consolidate, and consequently, this intensive period of learning may demand a great deal of sleep."

Specifically, rapid eye movement (REM) sleep is most important for memory consolidation and storage during sleep. There has been debate in recent years about just how important it is to memory, but sleep can also serve another purpose— we sleep to forget the unimportant facets of our day and filter them out so our memories can be more organized.

In 2003, research conducted at the University of Wisconsin-Madison hypothesized that neurons and synapses essentially worked and proliferated in overload during the day and were pruned back during sleep so only the important things made it into longer-term memory. This implies that we sleep to literally forget certain parts of our day and to have better-organized memory.

A team of researchers from the University of Rochester has also posited that sleep is like the brain's "waste removal system." When you can provide the systems responsible for memory a reprieve overnight, it is simply likely they will continue to work better for you in the coming days.

Sleep can serve many specific purposes on the brain and memory, but overall, the brain, like the body, needs rest and recovery. This is not even mentioning the deleterious effects of sleep deprivation, where one set of researchers from the University of California, Los Angeles, likened a lack of sleep to drinking too much. Patients with epilepsy were studied, and they were found to have a litany of ongoing issues: memory lapses, distorted visual perception, impaired and sluggish thought, and a slow reaction time. From the description alone, it sounds like someone who has had a few too many alcoholic drinks. Think of sleep as ongoing maintenance for the machine of your brain.

The final piece of the puzzle is exercise. It might be surprising to hear that physical exercise is just as good for your brain as it is for your muscles and bones, but it's been proven time and time again.

One particular study was conducted at Radboud University in the Netherlands. Male and female subjects took a memory test, and then one-third of them exercised immediately after the test, one-third of them exercised four hours after the test, and the remaining third did not exercise after the test. The subjects were collected two days later to repeat the same memory test, and the group who exercised four hours after the initial test performed the best without fail. It appeared that exercise was effective in helping the brain stabilize and store the memory.

Other studies take the physiological angle and point to the neurotransmitters and hormones that exercise releases and how they affect memory processes. Exercise is instrumental in the production of a brain protein called FNDC5, which eventually releases brain-derived neurotrophic factor (BDNF). BDNF has been shown to aid general brain functioning and memory processing by preserving existing brain cells, promoting new brain cells, and promoting overall brain growth. Human brains tend to shrink when we grow older, but exercise, which creates BDNF, can literally increase the size of your brain.

The presence of BDNF is especially supportive of long-term memory. Most BDNF activity occurs in the brain areas most correlated with high-level cognition, learning, and recall—namely, the hippocampus, cortex, and basal forebrain. BDNF can also help proper sleep regulation and (though this is not a promise) can curb excessive appetite, which could lead to marginal amounts of weight loss. Conversely, the *lack* of BDNF can cause depression, and people suffering from Parkinson's disease tend to have low levels of the protein.

Researcher Joyce Gomes-Osman reviewed studies that associated exercise with different brain functions. Her goal was to find what "doses" of exercise were most effective for certain types of cognitive function. While Gomes-Osman stressed that there wasn't a specific "magic number" that will unfailingly promote greater brain function, she did determine that elderly people who managed one hour of exercise three days per week showed the greatest improvement in brain functioning and speed.

Your brain has the highest oxygen requirement of any organ in your body, up to 20% of your entire body's usage. When you can exercise and improve your cardiovascular systems and ensure that blood is pumping better through your arteries, you will have greater access to oxygen. It's the same with water—the brain is, on average, 70% composed of water, and exercise makes you more aware of hydration.

Exercise does have its limits, however. The best types of exercise are those that increase blood flow and burn fat. If exercise becomes too strenuous and difficult, then you begin to create stress, and you've already read how detrimental stress can be on your mental faculties. Overall, it appears that the maxim of healthy body, healthy mind holds very true.

It's just another case of why we should have listened to our mothers more when we were young.

Sleep as much as possible, exercise often, and don't sweat the small things. When we can avoid the stressors in our life, we can devote more mental bandwidth to that which matters. You wouldn't be great at studying for a test if your dog was missing, would you? We can better comprehend and understand difficult material when we have a full night's sleep. Finally, exercise is not only invigorating and important for giving you a mental break, but it can cause chemical changes in the brain that benefit your memory processes. The brain is the engine of learning and expertise, and you have to be mindful of priming it for optimal performance.

Takeaways:

- Neural growth is anything but easy. In fact, by definition, easy tasks don't really cause any growth. Think of the brain as the earth being shaped by rivers and lakes. Now that's a process that takes time and effort.
- Thus, the first principle to increasing neuroplasticity is about stimulation. You need more of it, as much as you can get in your daily life. Learning is one of the primary forms of mental stimulation. You essentially need to avoid passive

activities and engage your brain and make it work.

- Second, enriched environments help create neuroplasticity because they offer you no other choice. Imagine being dropped into a foreign country—you would probably learn the language of that country pretty quickly out of necessity. Thus, there are specific ways in which you can design the various environments of your life to aid stimulation and challenge. Not the most pleasant or comfortable way of living, but the most effective.

- Third, persistence and consistency. The Grand Canyon wasn't carved in a day, and neither will the neural connections that you wish to cultivate. To jump to yet another analogy, think of how you might approach a gym workout. You can have more sets, use heavier weights, go more frequently, or have a longer workout in general. Those are the ways that the brain grows as well.

- Fourth, the brain is not an ethereal entity. It has a physical basis for functioning, and it is mostly based on sleep, exercise, fuel, and stress (or the lack thereof). If you can't take care of your physical self, you can't expect your brain to perform very well.

Chapter 4. The Neuroscience of Yes and No

So far, we've discussed changing your brain in terms of structural and functional plasticity—the science behind creating and strengthening neural connections and taking over parts of the brain that aren't being used in the cortical remapping manner, respectively. Both cases create real, physical change inside the brain. We've mostly discussed structural plasticity because that's what we can seek to influence on a daily basis. Structural neuroplasticity underlies our learning, habits, and patterns of behavior.

This chapter takes a slightly different approach to changing and molding the brain for good, as we delve a bit deeper into other agents of neural change, notably *neurotransmitters*, the chemical substances that dictate our feelings and thoughts, versus the actual physical structures of the brain.

It is a slight distinction, but they are virtually incapable of being discussed separately as they both create the same end result of patterns of behavior that are hard to create and also hard to break out of.

You could also argue that this chapter still addresses structural neuroplasticity because neural changes all have some physical basis, and the fact that some neurotransmitters are produced more than others is a reflection of those neural grooves that have been created over time. Here, they have produced strengthened neurotransmitter pathways and increased or dulled the sensitivity of corresponding receptors. There has been a neural groove worn to inhibit or encourage these chemicals.

In the case of this chapter, we are focusing on the neuroplasticity that dictates our "yes" and "no" responses. The yes response is something that we want to empower and strengthen, as it's what tells us that "Yes, we can" achieve and do. This is related to self-discipline, motivation, and defeating procrastination. Thus, the neurotransmitters of "yes" are the ones that we rely on to spark us into action; we want more of them because they allow us to translate our intentions into action.

Manipulating the neuroplasticity of yes is how you can go to the gym even when you're exhausted and it's raining outside. It's the feeling that you can delay gratification and exercise willpower to accomplish a greater goal. These feelings are made possible, if not driven by, the neuroscience of yes.

On the other hand, the no response is something that holds us back from what we want. This is related to anxiety and fear and the instinctual desire for safety. Thus, the neurotransmitters of "no" are set up to *stop* us from taking action, preferring a lack of motion or even retreat. This keeps us from our goals, and we generally want to overcome them and minimize their production.

The neuroplasticity of no is what keeps you from raising your hand in class or is the feeling in the pit of your stomach before you step onto a stage to speak to five hundred people. These are irrational feelings of stress and fear, and they ultimately hold you back from your best intentions. The neuroscience of no comes from our evolutionary drive for survival and safety, without regard to the reality of situations.

In this chapter, we'll learn about the mechanisms that lead to us to have stronger yes or no responses and how to control them to produce the behavior and habits that you want—usually a more powerful yes response and a weakened no response. As with all things in neuroscience, it's a matter of battling your subconscious routines that have slowly worn grooves into your brain and introducing new ones through repetition and presence.

The Neuroscience of Yes: Motivation, Discipline, and Focus

How does the motivated brain work? What's different on a biological level in someone who has a strong yes response in all areas of life? It's the neurotransmitters—how they are produced, processed, and received.

Motivation is especially tied to a specific neurotransmitter: dopamine. Dopamine, or the lack thereof, is also what underlies our willpower and sense of self-discipline.

Dopamine is one of the agents that work on the brain's pleasure and reward centers. It's especially tied to the mesolimbic pathway, the most vital reward pathway in the human brain. This pathway extends to various other parts of the brain, including a spot called the nucleus accumbens. This particular region is another center for the rewards circuit. And oh does the brain respond to rewards, instant gratification, and pleasure like nothing else.

When we experience pleasure or a reward of some type, dopamine is usually at the root of it—the greater the amount of dopamine released, the greater the pleasure we feel. It happens during and after a pleasurable event—you feel it *while* you are eating a dozen donuts and also *after* you finish a great workout at the gym. However, dopamine is also released in *anticipation* of pleasure or reward, which ties it directly to motivation. And of course, chasing dopamine for the present moment instead of pushing it off is what happens when we lose self-discipline.

If you start feeling good in anticipation of something, chances are you will be motivated into action to seek more of it. Thus, the more dopamine flying around in your system, the more motivated we will be.

But it's not just the amount of dopamine that influences how motivated we are to capture pleasure. The influence of dopamine on your motivation also hinges upon *where* dopamine is present in the human brain. Scientists from Vanderbilt

University examined the brains of both highly motivated and unmotivated people. They found that go-getters secreted higher levels of dopamine in their striatum and prefrontal cortex, regions of the brain that correlate to movement and decision-making.

The "slackers," on the other hand, had an excess of dopamine in the anterior insula, which is more connected to consciousness and subjective feelings. This is to say that "slackers" get more pleasure and comfort from not doing anything, physically at least, while go-getters physically gain more pleasure from acting. Happiness either goes hand-in-hand with action or the lack thereof. You may not be able to determine exactly where the dopamine levels in your brain are located, but you *can* easily control the amount you have in your brain at all times.

This seems to boil *biological* motivation down to a simple recipe (*psychological* motivation is a whole other story).

If dopamine spikes are the causes of motivation and discipline, then it stands to reason the more often we can provide the brain with rewards, the more likely we'll be motivated to overrule our laziness and spur ourselves to action. And science suggests there are ways we can, in fact, generate more dopamine going to the right places.

The more instances of dopamine production we can generate, the more our brains will be trained to make us more motivated. So one suggestion is to keep the brain in a constant state of either receiving rewards or in anticipation of rewards. Since things as small as scrolling through social media can generate dopamine, this is easier than we think.

For instance, you can set incredibly incremental goals with accompanying rewards at each turn. When you achieve a goal, you bask in the anticipation of the reward you set aside for yourself, as well as gain the pleasure of accomplishment when you finish it.

Dopamine's role in reinforcing pleasure correlates to one of the most well-known theories concerning human behavior. Rather, perhaps it's more accurate to say that the studies on dopamine align with this more foundational theory.

Out of all the speculations about the sources of motivation, none is more famous than the *pleasure principle*. The reason it's so renowned is because it's also the easiest to understand. The pleasure principle was first raised in public consciousness by the father of psychoanalysis, Sigmund Freud, though researchers as far back as Aristotle in ancient Greece noted how easily we could be manipulated and motivated by pleasure and pain.

The pleasure principle asserts that the human mind does everything it can to seek out pleasure and avoid pain. It doesn't get simpler than that. In that simplicity, we find some of life's most universal and predictable motivators.

The pleasure principle is employed by the *id*, which is how Freud identifies one of the psyche's three governing entities (the others being the ego and the superego). For our purposes, we'll focus only on the id. The id houses our desires and physical "needs." It doesn't have any sense of restraint. It is primal and unfiltered. It goes after whatever it can to meet our body's urges for happiness and fulfillment. Anything that causes pleasure is felt by the brain the same way, whether it's a tasty meal or a drug. An apt comparison, in fact, is a drug addict who will stop at nothing to get another taste of narcotics.

There are a few rules that govern the pleasure principle and how we are motivated.

Every decision we make is based on gaining pleasure or avoiding pain. This is the common motivation for every person on earth. No matter what we do in the course of our day, it all gets down to the pleasure principle. You raid the refrigerator for snacks because you crave the taste and feel of certain food. You get a haircut because you think it will make you more attractive to someone else, which will make you happy, which is pleasure.

Conversely, you wear a protective mask while you're using a blowtorch because you want to avoid sparks flying into your face and eyes, because that will be painful. If you trace all of our decisions back, whether short-term or long-term, you'll find that they all stem from a small set of pleasures or pains.

People work harder to avoid pain than to get pleasure. While everyone wants pleasure as much as they can get it, their motivation to avoid pain is actually far stronger. The instinct to survive a threatening situation is more immediate than eating your favorite candy bar, for instance. So when faced with the prospect of pain, the brain will work harder than it would to gain access to pleasure.

For example, imagine you're standing in the middle of a desert road. In front of you is a treasure chest filled with money and outlandishly expensive jewelry that could set you up financially for the rest of your life. But there's also an out-of-control semi careening toward it. You're probably going to make the decision to jump away from the truck rather than grab the treasure chest, because your instinct to avoid pain—in this case, certain death—outweighed your desire to gain pleasure.

If you've hit rock bottom and faced a massive amount of pain or displeasure, then you simply must start acting to avoid that in the future. A wounded animal is more motivated than a slightly uncomfortable one.

Our perceptions of pleasure and pain are more powerful drivers than the actual things. When our brain is judging between what will be a pleasant or painful experience, it's working from scenarios that we *think* could result if we took a course of action. In other words, our *perceptions* of pleasure and pain are really what's driving the car. And sometimes those perceptions can be flawed. In fact, they are mostly flawed, which explains our tendency to work against our own best interests.

I can think of no better example of this rule than jalapeño chapulines. They're a spicy, traditional Mexican snack that's tasty and low in carbs. By the way, "chapulines" means "grasshoppers." We're talking chili-flavored grasshoppers. The insects.

Now, you may have no firsthand knowledge of how grasshoppers taste. Maybe you've never tried them. But the *thought* of eating grasshoppers may give you pause. You imagine they'll be repellant to the tongue. You imagine if you take a bite of a grasshopper you'll get grossed out. You might accidentally bite down on an internal grasshopper organ. The *perception* of eating a grasshopper is driving you quickly away from the act of eating one.

But the fact remains that *you haven't actually tried it yet*. You're working from your *idea* of the repulsion that eating a grasshopper will bring about. Somebody who's actually tried grasshopper-based cuisine may insist to you that they're really *good* when prepared properly. Still, you might not be able to get over your innate perception of what eating an insect would be like.

Pleasure and pain are changed by time. In general, we focus on the here and now: what can I get very soon that will bring me happiness? Also, what is coming up very soon that could be intensely painful that I'll have to avoid? When considering the attainment of comfort, we're more tuned in to what might happen immediately. The pleasure and pain that might happen months or years from now doesn't really register with us—what's most important is whatever's right at our doorstep. Of course, this is another way in which our perceptions are flawed and why we might procrastinate so frequently.

For example, a smoker needs a cigarette. It's the main focus of their current situation. It brings them a certain relief or pleasure. And in about fifteen minutes, they'll be on break so they can enjoy that cigarette. It's the focus of their daily ritual. They're *not* thinking about how smoking a cigarette every time they "need" one could cause painful health problems down the road.

That's a distant reality that's not driving them at all. Right now, they need a smoke because they crave one, and they might get a headache immediately if they don't get one.

Emotion beats logic. When it comes to the pleasure principle, your feelings tend to overshadow rational thought. You might know that doing something will be good or bad for you. You'll understand all the reasons why it will be good or bad. You'll get all that. But if your illogical id is so intent on satisfying a certain craving, then it's probably going to win out. And if your id drives you to think that doing something useful will cause too much stress or temporary dissatisfaction, it's going to win there too.

Going back to our smoker, without a doubt they know why cigarettes are bad for one's health. They've read those warnings on the packages. Maybe in school they saw a picture of a corroded lung that resulted from years of smoking. They *know* all the risks they're about to court. But there's that pack right in front of them. And all reason be damned, they're going to have that cigarette. Their emotions oriented toward pleasure win out.

Survival overrides everything. When our survival instinct gets activated, everything else in our psychological and emotional makeup turns off. If a life-threatening situation (or a *perceived* life-threatening situation) arises in our existence, the brain closes down everything else and turns us into a machine whose thoughts and actions are all oriented toward the will to survive.

This shouldn't be surprising when it comes to avoiding painful outcomes. Of *course* you're going to try and jump away from that oncoming semi truck; if you don't, you won't survive. Your system won't let you make that choice—it's going to do everything it can to get you the hell out of the way of that truck.

However, survival can *also* come into play when we're seeking pleasure—even if it means we might slip into harm's way. The most obvious example of this is food. Say you're at a bar and somebody orders a giant plate of nachos loaded with cheese, sour cream, fatty meat, and a bunch of other things that might not be the best dietary choices for you. You *might* be able to resist it. Some people can. But you might not. In fact, you could find yourself eating half the plate before you even know what you've done.

Why? Because you need food to survive. And your brain is telling you there's food in the vicinity, so perhaps you should eat it. Never mind that it's not the best kind of food, nutritionally speaking, that you could opt for at the moment. Your survival instinct is telling you it's time to have those nachos. Your life depends on it.

Our brain chemistry is working from these two very basic opposites of pain and pleasure, and some of the circuitry involved has been strengthened or warped by our life experiences. But it's possible to put these rules, and the pleasure principle in general, to work in ways that will increase your motivation and overall yes response.

The Inhibition System

What's known as the brain inhibition system also contributes to our ability to regulate ourselves and push our brains into a state of yes. Normally, we would associate inhibition with preventing us from taking an action. But the brain's inhibition system actually assists us because it inhibits *distracting* thoughts and helps us focus on a task at hand or one that is being planned.

This can be demonstrated by a series of trials called the Stroop test, named after the psychologist who first discovered the effect it recalls. In these tests, participants were given a set of cards that contained "color" words—but the actual color of the text was in a different color than the word itself. For example, the word "green" would be in red text, the word "purple" would be in green-colored text, and so on. The test-takers were told to express what color the text was actually in, not the word itself. So when a volunteer was shown the word "blue" but the text itself was colored red, the correct answer would be "red."

Researchers found that it took the brain a whole lot of effort to give the correct answer—the actual color of the text itself. That is, the brain had to inhibit its natural inclination and think more than usual. The brain is much more aligned and comfortable in reading the text straight. In order to give the correct answer of the color itself, the neural system has to work overtime (relatively speaking) to keep the respondent from reading the word and give the color, which in this case is the slightly more abstract concept.

The word is much easier to read because it's unambiguous and conveys a straighter message. The brain has to inhibit itself from reading the word before it says the color of the word, and this is a draining activity. Parsing through distractions is tough!

The neural structures involved in inhibition are called the ventrolateral prefrontal cortices—but we'll *inhibit* ourselves from calling it that and abbreviate it to the VLPFC. These structures are located next to our left and right temples in the prefrontal cortex. How well you can maintain focus and ignore distractions is directly correlated to how well you control the VLPFC.

What's more, the VLPFC is the *only* part of the brain that inhibits acknowledging additional stimuli (in other words, distractions), whereas there are a *lot* more structures in the brain that push us to notice everything around us and thus become distracted and leave our intentions behind. The VLPFC is the earplug, while other structures act as undesired hearing aids.

When it comes to staying on target and exercising self-discipline, all we've got is the VLPFC. This means once we've got it in our minds to veer off target or simply get distracted, this neural loop is difficult to break. As we've seen, once dopamine makes up its mind, it can override every inhibiting factor in its path with its momentum and desire for pleasure or gratification. In fact, the *arousal* itself is kind of its own reward.

When that starts rolling, it's extremely difficult to stop it. And our so-called braking system is fragile and temperamental and isn't entirely reliable. This leads us to one very important realization in allowing yourself to say yes to what you want: you need to deal with distractions that rob you of your inhibitory powers *before* they take hold.

When you're supposed to be researching for a project, you have to stop the urge to gaze upon social media or play video games *before* those urges have driven you off course. It also has to happen in relatively short order, because if you wait too long, the dopamine is just going to bully its way through and ask why you aren't indulging yourself in pleasure.

The key to helping the VLPFC work at its best, therefore, is timing. You have to try and stop the distractions before they start. Doing so requires that you become hyper-aware of your own proclivities: monitoring where your attention goes, understanding when the urge to be distracted happens, and turning everything that's distracting you off as much as possible. No one said it was going to be easy!

The Neuroscience of Pumping Yourself Up

Your brain, as we've discussed in earlier chapters, shapes itself based on whatever it sees or is exposed to—whether it's real or imagined. If you say (or even just think), "I'm going to finish a decathlon in record time," the brain treats it no differently than if you *actually* finish a decathlon in record time. Your neural pathways are reshaping themselves based on your declaration alone. Now that's helpful to the neuroscience of yes.

Most of the time, this works against us when we have a negative dialogue with ourselves about our flaws and probability of failing. However, like all things neurological, it is neutral and can be harnessed to your benefit. To effect neuroplasticity, you only need to state your intent, verbally or mentally. The brain simply can't distinguish between an act and a thought if the thought is present and conscious enough. It's akin to the very real fact that a person going through the breakup of a romantic relationship has brain activity in the same areas where physical pain would register.

Self-talk can have dramatic and unexpected effects. The Lerner Research Institute conducted a study in which participants were told to form mental pictures of themselves flexing their pinky fingers and elbows. Others were instructed to physically do the flexing. After 12 weeks the group doing the physical flexes showed a 53% increase in their finger strength—but the groups that only did the mental work showed increases of between 13% and 35%.

This fact has huge significance when it comes to the act of self-talk, the kind that will lift you out of an indifferent state and motivate you to get something accomplished. In fact, it doesn't have to strictly be *verbalized* talk: research has shown that our brains use the same neural networks to both move and just *think* about moving. Imagining a positive action or plan over and over again might not have an impact on our physical status, but it has a momentous effect on neuroplasticity. That mental groove can be worn without you lifting a single finger.

Physiologists also strongly suspect that self-talk can alter how you perceive yourself. Our senses are always giving us information about how our world is at any given moment: how it looks, sounds, feels, smells, and so forth. That information can be affected by our own cultural biases and what everybody else in our peer group might believe. But self-talk gives you a chance to literally reform your brain with your own standards, free from outside influence and perceptions. Say what you want your reality to be, and eventually, it will be true. And that can build your self-confidence to amazing levels.

How you talk to yourself is crucial as well—and psychologist Ethan Kross of the University of Michigan stumbled upon a potential trick that might sound a little precious but could also pay off in higher dividends: talking to yourself as if you're someone else, in the third person.

Kross found that when some people talk to themselves using the pronoun "I," they may be unconsciously creating more stress and strain on their psyches. Taking self-ownership infers a lot of responsibility and expectation, and that can make someone trying to effect change a little nervous. "I'm going to ace that entrance exam" or "I'm going to get through this family crisis with flying colors" are good things to say—but by using the word "I," the speaker may be putting more pressure on themselves.

Kross ran an experiment with volunteers in which they were all told they'd be giving a speech with only five minutes in which they could prepare themselves. While they were getting ready, he told some of the volunteers to talk to themselves using the pronoun "I." He asked the others either to address themselves as "you" or by their given names.

The "I" group tended to stress out, saying things like "I only have five minutes to get ready for this? I can't do it in five minutes! I'm going to be flailing up there!" The messages the "you" group said were very,

very different: "Patrick, you've got this. You've given speeches like this millions of times in the past. You'll come through fine."

These results point toward the idea that addressing yourself as a third person is somehow an objectivity enabler: it forces a perception upon you as an outsider, looking at your situation from a distance. In that framework, you're much more likely to see yourself as a problem-solver rather than a victim, and your statements of support are more likely to be positive, more rational, and less emotionally charged. In general, it makes you a nicer person to yourself. That change in wording alone could have a significant effect on your neural pathways.

For that reason, visualization is a big thing with successful athletes and public figures. Imagining an effect serves as a kind of affirmation, and when it's repeated hundreds or even thousands of times, your neural pathways are practically reconstructed to orient themselves with the outcome you desire. With all that mental self-talk and visualization, that outcome can happen much sooner than one might expect.

Visualization: Seeing Is Believing

A powerful tool that's often overlooked is *visualization*. This happens before you lift a finger and is something that you can repeat ad nauseam to build a stronger yes response.

Visualization, quite simply put, is *detailed imagination*. You use your mind's eye to picture yourself executing whatever it is you're planning to accomplish. Visualization helps you build a sense of awareness and expectation. It's a mental rehearsal to understand the experience and associated emotions.

And believe it or not, it works. Australian researcher Alan Richardson ran a trial on visualization on a group of basketball players. He divided them into three different groups and gave each a 20-day assignment involving free throws.

All of the groups physically practiced making free throws on the first and last days of the 20-day period. One group was instructed to practice making free throws for 20 minutes every day. A second group was instructed to do nothing in between the first and twentieth days.

Finally, a third group was told only to "visualize" themselves making free throws between the first and last days of the trials. This process didn't just mean the players pictured themselves sinking shots successfully—it also included visualizing their *missing* free throws and *practicing* correcting their shot.

The results were eye-opening. The group that physically practiced for 20 days boosted their free throw success rate by 24%. But astonishingly, the visualization group also improved by 23%—almost as much as the practice squad. Not surprisingly, the group that did neither didn't improve at all.

The conclusion from this study is that visualization causes changes even when unaccompanied by actual physical work. The brain and its neural pathways can be conditioned and strengthened, just as muscles and the cardiovascular system can. Visualization can help align the brain with the physical execution of anything we do and can be a great means of additional support in our efforts. Seeing is believing, no matter the type of seeing.

Use this tool to make yourself, well, whatever you want to be. For instance, visualize a situation you are afraid of and make all the tough, disciplined, and unpleasant choices in your mind. Play it through with as many details as possible. How does it feel? We can start to understand that our fear is rooted in ignorance, and we can start to build a relationship with the feeling of comfort with discomfort. Almost all of us hesitate and want to retreat to a comfort zone when confronted with something foreign. Make risky situations as familiar as possible and this instinct will decrease accordingly.

Visualization is easy, but as with any process, it works best with guided steps. It is helpful to approach visualization as meditation—a quiet but concentrated immersion into your thoughts and imagination. One particularly effective technique involves five steps.

1. Relaxation. The first step involves getting yourself into a tranquil state, physically and mentally. It involves techniques like finding a quiet spot, taking deep and measured breaths, and closing your eyes to get into a meditative state.

2. Imagining the environment. The second step is building a detailed mental picture of the situation, surroundings, and specific objects that you'll be working with when you finally take action.

3. Viewing as third person. The third part of this method is picturing yourself doing an activity the way someone else would—how you'd appear in the eyes of someone watching you.

4. Viewing as first person. The fourth part is an intensive imagining of yourself doing the activity—how your senses and emotions would react and feel while you're doing it.

5. Coming back to reality. The final part involves *slowly* reemerging from your visualization into the physical world, ready to take on the challenge for real.

Let's try a sample visualization with a situation that we frequently find ourselves in but can cause some to feel utter panic and terror about: delivering a speech. It doesn't seem as challenging as jumping out of an airplane or taking part in a sword fight, but some of the toughest people in the world have trepidation about standing in front of a group of polite people and speaking directly to them. Build your yes response and quiet your no response. Applying the above five steps, here's how that visualization might go.

1. Relax. Find a quiet spot where you won't be disturbed or interrupted for a few minutes—lying on a couch or bed with the windows and doors closed. Breathe deeply from your stomach. Take as much time as you need to let all areas of tension in your body dissipate. Finally, close your eyes.

2. Imagine the environment. Make a detailed survey of the room and space where you'll be making your speech. Picture the chairs the audience will sit in. Imagine the lighting and feel of the room, from how bright the overhead lamps might be to the air conditioning. Is the stage raised above the floor? Is there a podium you'll be standing behind? Will there be a microphone, or will you be wearing a headset? Imagine how either looks, down to the foam piece over the microphone head or the tiny earphones.

3. View as third person. Now you're somebody in the audience watching as you speak. You see yourself dressed in a suit, standing upright, delivering words clearly and directly, raising your pitch to make a point or lowering your pitch to make a joke. You're seeing all the hand gestures, head tilts, and facial expressions you'd see if you were watching the speech instead of giving it.

4. View as first person. At this point you go back into yourself, giving the speech and addressing the audience. You can hear how your words sound in your head. You note the distance from your mouth to the microphone. You can see the audience members' faces as they're paying attention. You hear the reverb from your voice echoing throughout the room, whether it's a little or a lot. You feel your hands resting on the wood surface of the podium. You see the words printed on the page you're reading from—or you see yourself moving around the stage without a script. You sense how your body's reacting: the nervous energy in your gut, the clarity in your head, the blood flow in your arms and legs. You hear the applause at the end, down to each individual handclap.

5. *Wrap it up.* You let the scene fade to black (or white if you prefer) in your head. You spend a few moments slowly coming back to, remembering the scene that's just transpired and marking each feeling you'll look out for when you're giving the speech. Recall specifically all the choices you made that were bold and daring as opposed to conservative and fearful. Then you gently open your eyes.

Somehow that visualization has made speech-giving seem terribly exciting. Imagine what it can do for parachuting and sword fighting.

We call the previously described process "visualization," but that phrasing isn't entirely accurate since most people associate visualization with seeing things with one's eyes. It happens. A more exact term for this process might be *multi-sensory imagination* or *mental rehearsal,* because the full process draws from all of the senses we possess:

Visual: sense of sight

Auditory: sense of hearing

Kinesthetic: sense of touch

Olfactory: sense of smell

Gustatory: sense of taste

It might be easiest for us to imagine visuals during mental rehearsal, but never underestimate the power of the other four senses, as well as emotional sensations. They're responsible for some of our strongest memories: the sound of a band, the smell of a rainy afternoon, the taste of an ice cream sundae, or the touch of a fuzzy sweater. During visualization, try as hard as you can to incorporate those other senses as well as how your scene looks to the eye.

Studies have shown that our brain chemistry treats imagined memories—visualization, that is—the same way as it treats *actual* memories. If you can visualize to a deep level, using all five senses and emotional projections, your brain is going to instill it as something you've already experienced. When you visualize jet-skiing, playing professional football, or being shot out of a cannon, your brain is just going to assume you've actually done so. You might logically know better, but emotionally you will be more even-keeled and calm, ready to tackle adversity.

This can be key in building your yes response. When you're about to do something you've never done before, most of the anxiety and tension you feel happens *before* you actually start doing it. The nervousness you feel in a new endeavor usually comes up when you're anticipating doing it. When you're actually doing it, most of that anxiety goes away.

Therefore, if the brain treats visualization the same way it treats real memories, you can trick your brain into building a belief in yourself. Sure, you might only be *visualizing* sky-diving, but if you do it thoroughly enough, your brain is going to understand that the fear that leads to a no response isn't necessary or even helpful.

The Neuroscience of No: Fear and Anxiety

Remember our limbic system from a few chapters back? Within it are the neural components that direct our "fight-or-flight" responses and how we react to real or perceived threats. Its purpose is to keep us alive and breathing. It makes us prioritize survival and security over everything else, and in doing so it holds us back from action. It tells us no—prematurely or with false alarms most of the time. Are you *really* in danger when you raise your hand to speak in a crowded room, or is it just your limbic system kicking in and elevating your heart rate?

Thus, the neuroscience of no is when fear and anxiety hijack the brain and prevent us from doing what we want. This is perhaps the deepest neural groove that exists, as it's been digging itself for thousands, if not millions, of years.

The limbic system, especially the hippocampus, is the network that deals with immediate and emotional responses. The amygdala, which is tied to all the other structures in the limbic system, is the primary driver of memories that are associated with anxiety and stress: those with high anxiety dysfunction typically have extraordinarily high activity in their amygdalae.

This is a response that is hardwired in all of us, but it is a neural pathway that can become even more powerful in some of us. Creating this neural groove to resort to fear and anxiety at the prospect of anything foreign can be quite easy.

For instance, fears typically start from childhood, when there was no logical voice to impart calm. Most anxiety disorders also start when people are young, which leads to even stronger and more innate neural wiring.

When we are children, our repeated exposure to fear and anxiety has its strongest effect on our neural pathways, especially in the ventrolateral prefrontal cortex and the hysterical amygdala. A highly anxious person who tends to focus or obsess on their condition also experiences alteration in the cingulate and insular cortices.

The rapid physical growth we experience as adolescents and teenagers corresponds with the development of our neural networks, especially when it comes to how we think, act, and feel—just as we're starting to shed all the neural pathways we *don't* use and shore up the ones we do. It's during this point that adverse neural development can cause serious damage to us, resulting in disorders that can last long into adulthood.

As a result, we may have negative neural pathways ingrained in us that we're overly used to. Our synaptic firings have been shaped and grooved so it's easier for us to reject situations that can cause anxiety and fear; we just work from our initial instinct because it's strong in our minds. It's important to remember this can be both good and bad: while our brain chemistry can keep us out of emotionally destructive situations, it can also keep us from positive happenings that might end well.

For example, maybe one might not feel up to getting on a treadmill and working out because they associate activity with an accident they might have had when they were younger. For whatever reason, the amygdala has classified physical activity as a potentially threatening or dangerous thing. The neural pathway that forms a negative response to physical movement is grooved and extremely easy for a neural message to travel down.

Fear is hardwired into everyone's brain for a good reason. Feeling fear is a natural part of being human. It is not abnormal, nor is it a sign of weakness. In fact, the ability to experience fear is a perfectly normal aspect of brain function. The lack of fear may actually be a sign of serious brain damage.

When a person feels fear, there are two primary pathways within the brain fear can take. One path is subconscious, implicit, and almost instantaneous. This is the primary pathway. The other path is conscious, explicit, and much, much slower. Of course, this is the secondary pathway.

The primary pathway is associated with the amygdala within the brain. When a person senses danger, the amygdala takes over and instantly discharges patterns to activate the body's fear circuits, which in turn release stress hormones of cortisol and adrenaline. This causes an increase in heart rate and blood pressure. Additional physiological responses include sweaty hands, dry mouth, and tense muscles.

This is the perfect response in many dangerous situations because it prepares the body to respond to a threat by either standing up to it or running away from it (fight or flight). When the blood flow is diverted quickly from the digestive area, the face, head, and neck, then it can be used elsewhere. And while a fist fight or a sprint from the situation is not often necessary in this modern world, the brain and body prepare just for those possible reactions. This is the reason people experience a racing heart and shortness of breath after being frightened.

The secondary and explicit pathway is the more thoughtful way we deal with a frightening stimulus.

Rather than being directed by the amygdala, this response is directed by the hippocampus, which is the structure within the brain that supports explicit or conscious memory. The hippocampus also provides context for the human experience. For example, it is the hippocampus that allows people to learn about and assess their surroundings in order to determine the levels of threat or friendliness. Additionally, the hippocampus is particularly sensitive to encoding the context associated with an aversive or painful experience.

The hippocampus is particularly active when people experience trauma within relationships. It only takes a small amount of fear stimulus for the hippocampus to condition a person to associate a particular stimulus with a conditioned fear. Additionally, objects and/or locations associated with the fear can also become a source of conditioned fear. This is how painful memories from old relationships can become generalized or projected into new ones.

An example of the hippocampus at work can be seen perpetuating the cycle of fear within families where shouting and yelling were predominant forms of punishment. A young girl comes to associate persistent screaming, racket, and hollering with family pain and chaos. As an adult, when her boyfriend or husband yells at her, she associates that ruckus with the family pain she experienced as a child. Therefore, when an argument starts and he raises his voice, her response is much like it was as a child: fight, run, or remain stuck in fright.

The primary response is automatic and happens with little thought, and this causes us to leap *before* we look. The secondary response that runs through the hippocampus is slower and can range from seconds to minutes of processing. Unlike the child whose upbringing is surrounded by constant shouting and screaming, a child who is yelled at for darting into the street without looking both ways is not going to associate raised voices with chaos and family pain that eventually leads to a fright response when her husband speaks loudly to her. The purpose of this book is to teach readers to deal with both types of responses to fear.

Fear also produces physiological changes, a few of which we have mentioned. When a person perceives a fear stimulus, adrenaline prepares the skeletal muscles to deal with whatever decision is made—fight or flight. Blood flows toward the body parts need to run away or pull the fists and fight it out.

However, there can be complications associated with these reactions.

First, if the blood flows away from the brain too quickly, then there are several possible reactions, none of which help with the fight-or-flight response. A person could faint, feel numbness, or freeze. At the most basic human survival level, this reaction is unlikely to end with a positive result. Even in our modern society, however, fainting during a stressful event, feeling numb and unsure of a response when given shocking news, or freezing up before making an important announcement are not conducive to reducing fears.

Second, when the body produces adrenaline in preparation for a physical fight-or-flight response, and then there is no vigorous physical activity after that arousal, uncomfortable physiological changes can occur. For example, many people experience sensations including trembling in their arms or legs, general weakness, or a heightened awareness of breathing and heart rate. If the adrenaline goes unused, imagine how you might feel after having four cups of coffee.

What if that happens time after time and a person cannot flee (run away) or fight (face the fear stimulus)? Those biological urges can become hardwired and habitual. Physically, the body has prepared to do something drastic, but what happens if those intentions or actions are never taken? These urges to flee or fight, these actions that were never taken, can get triggered repeatedly, especially when old, unresolved fear and hurt from the past are triggered by relationships in the present.

These can emerge as transference reactions or projections onto others. Furthermore, they could drive reenactment patterns that cause people to repeat the same mistakes in relationship after relationship in spite of their desire and commitment to avoid such blunders.

The biology of fear seems destined to only affect us in negative ways, but the truth is, we needed to have intense fear reactions to stay alive for most of human history. We are now in the business of deprogramming our brains of instinct, which is even more deeply ingrained than habit. It's a difficult but necessary road.

Certainly, major parts of fear are through instinct, but there are also *learned* and *taught* aspects. Instinctual fears are those things that are feared in order to ensure survival. From the beginning of time, mankind has feared large beasts because of the threat they pose to survival. In the modern world, people might fear dirty-looking food because they are worried about contracting a particular disease or disorder.

Recognize that fear has many helpful roles in life. Without a healthy sense of fear, humans would not have made it to this point on the evolutionary trail. Even in this modern age, fear can be our lighthouse in the dark seas.

Fear serves as a **protector.** When a person is afraid of something, it is often for good reason. What they fear could have both the power and the potential to bring harm. When the brain identifies a threat, the hypothalamus is triggered, thus letting the rest of the body know how best to prepare for whatever might be coming.

Afterward, the adrenal glands release adrenaline to alert the nervous system that it is time to get into survival mode (either fight or flight). Another hormone, norepinephrine, is also released during this period. Its purpose is to improve focus while reducing panic. Jake Deutsch, MD, an emergency room physician, says norepinephrine "allows clearer thinking under stress, which is precisely why it's used in many antidepressants." Thus, being in a panicky situation is far more likely to help someone think quickly and clearly than chugging another energy drink or reaching for a triple espresso latte.

Who can forget the Miracle on the Hudson? In 2009, Captain Chesley B. Sullivan landed a plane filled with 155 passengers and crew in the middle of the Hudson River in New

York City after birds damaged the engines. With all those lives in his hands, "Sully" was able to remain calm under extreme pressure and land safely. His ability to focus all of his energy into saving that plane prevented a terrible disaster.

Fear serves as a **motivator**. University certainly brings out the "fear as motivator" theme like few other life experiences. At one time, in the not so distant past, it meant sliding the final paper into the assignment slot in the English Department office before 8:00 a.m. on the last day of class. Now students upload the drafts to the portal by 11:59 p.m. or hit send just as the deadline approaches. The technology may have changed, but students have not. And nothing lights the motivational fires like the looming deadline of semester's end.

It is not just on campus, however, that fear motivates. There's this old joke. The new guy asks his mentor, "How long have you worked here?" The mentor answers, "I've been here 10 years, but I started working last month when they threatened to fire me." And while it is a knee-slapper at motivational conventions worldwide, there is a lot of truth in it. Fear can be an incredible motivator, especially when you're trying to accomplish career and workplace goals.

Debbie Mandel, stress-management specialist and the author of *Addicted to Stress*, says an adrenaline rush not only helps you delegate and become a productive team member, but it also is needed by many during the "eleventh hour, whether it's to tackle a project at work or write a paper on a deadline."

Finally, fear is your **analyst**. Fear does not show up in life without reason. Typically, there is a fear that needs tackling, and the only way to do so is to face it head-on. If you're experiencing fear, it does you good to ask what is causing it and for what purpose. In life, thoughts of failure or loss naturally cause people to do everything possible to avoid those experiences.

Sometimes the only way to avoid becoming a victim of a fear is to analyze the fear. Asking questions like "What am I actually afraid of?" and "What can I do to overcome this fear?" allows people to work through the obstacles that hold them back while looking for new ways to take proactive steps in a new direction.

Conquering a strong no response doesn't simply require beefing up your yes response. After all, if you have a river that flows the wrong direction, you can't just dig a new canal for the water. You have to redirect the water's path completely to make sure it flows where you want. That's a mental process that consists of something called cognitive behavioral therapy, which is the process of changing thought patterns.

Rewiring the No Response

Our thoughts and beliefs are instilled at an early age and reinforced by our experiences. Changing or rewiring these neural grooves that you may not even be aware of is difficult, but there is a guided process that simplifies the change.

Challenging and changing them from an analytical perspective is what is known as cognitive behavioral therapy, or CBT for short. The main strategy of CBT is to teach people how to deal with their negative core beliefs, head-on, and reprogram them into something less harmful. In our context, it's to rewire the neural pathways of the no response that are sabotaging you. The main method to do so is called *cognitive restructuring*—a technique for identifying negative thought patterns and altering them. In other words, turning a no into a yes.

By recognizing a negative thought pattern and understanding why it persists, we can react differently to it and steer ourselves in a positive direction. For instance, just about any phobia is grounded in some type of primal fear. You can certainly fall off a staircase and break your neck, but you're not likely to. Thus, is your heightened fear of heights serving you well or causing you unnecessary stress and anxiety?

You may not be able to help it, but that's where CBT comes in to replace your instinctual, subconscious thoughts with empowering, positive ones. This is how you can battle back against the limbic system and amygdala from running the show and allow your prefrontal cortex to step in and dictate a more logical course of action. That's how you begin to change your thoughts from the physical level.

Few people are actively aware of their thinking patterns, even though they engage in these patterns every day. CBT allows you to address errors in your thinking to correct your behavior and in turn change your life. You might assume that you require a therapist or at least an incredibly patient friend to conduct CBT, but that's where thought diaries and worksheets come into play.

The concept of the thought diary was borne from the desire to identify the core beliefs that inform our actions and emotions. It uncovers the relationships between our behavior, thoughts, and feelings. It's how you see exactly what neural paths you have and how you define the neural path that you want.

A typical entry in a thought diary outlines a triggering event or thought, the self-messaging that comes from it, and the resultant emotions that emerge. Sifting through all this information brings up your beliefs so you can challenge them. Remember, we want to try to isolate and analyze the automatic thoughts we have and replace them with healthier versions.

Steps in a thought diary entry can be arranged in the easy-to-remember A-C-B format.

Activating event. This is the origin point of your emotional change. This is what caused you to spiral into fear or anxiety. It could be an actual, physical event. But it could also be an internal event—a thought, memory, or mental image. It's whatever caused your emotional status to change from calm to agitation:

- running into an old friend on the street

- being criticized by a supervisor

- remembering being bullied by a high school classmate

Consequences. In this step you identify the specific emotions and sensations that arose. These could be simple feeling words— "anxious," "unhappy," "sickened," "panicky," "melancholy," "confused," and so forth. To get more specific about the emotions involved, you may want to rate how intensely you felt them on whatever scale works for you. Maybe you were 65% panicky and 35% confused. Your feelings of sickness may have been a 10 and your anxiety may have been a 5. Underline or circle which emotion was most relevant.

Beliefs. This is where the action begins. How do you link the activating event with the consequences? What unconscious narrative or story about yourself was told to achieve the consequence? What leaps in logic or conclusions were being made to get you to your current negative state? Getting to the bottom of these beliefs involves some drilling of yourself with progressive questioning until you finally get to the bottom of your situation—your core beliefs:

- "What was I thinking?"

- "What was going through my head when this happened?"

- "What's wrong with that?"

- "What does this all mean?"

- "What does it reveal about me?"

Yes, it's a lot of work, and you might struggle at points to obtain the answers you're looking for. But the effort to peel away layers of self-messaging will eventually pay off. When your investigation finally brings you face-to-face with your core beliefs, that's when you can start the process of challenging them.

Let's take an example of a seemingly benign activating event and put it through the A-C-B ringer.

1. Steve is having a conversation with his new friend Emily at a table. They're having a good talk until Steve's acquaintance Jack walks up, pulls up a chair, and starts chatting, oblivious to the fact that he stopped

Steve and Emily's conversation cold. Steve is angry. You won't like him when he is angry.

Steve's activating event is Jack stopping his conversation. That's easy.

What is the consequence—what did this event activate, feelings-wise? He felt flustered, for one. That was probably the dominant emotion. He'd give it an 8 on a scale of 1–10. He also sensed a feeling of anger and frustration, but not quite as powerfully as the panic. Maybe a 4. He felt the front of his head get a little heavy. Steve qualifies that as "confusion." But he's not sure why, so he gives it a 3.

Now Steve has to figure out why this particular event made him freak out. Does he dislike Jack? No, not at all, he decides. He's an okay guy, if sometimes a little over-excitable.

So Steve asks himself what was going through his head at the time. He was having a good conversation with Emily, feeling like they were both talking earnestly and actively about things they're both interested in. And then it got interrupted. He felt flustered.

Why? Because he was disappointed that the conversation was derailed and that Jack wasn't self-aware enough to know he was interrupting.

What does that mean? He feels that Jack was being careless about his ego and personality and thought nothing of imposing his will over Jack's.

Why is that? Because Steve doesn't think he asserts himself enough.

And why is that? Because Steve believes he's too modest to ever be able to do that.

And what does that mean? Steve doesn't feel he deserves respect, and Jack's interruption was just a reminder that he doesn't deserve it.

That's Steve's core belief: he has little if any self-regard and thinks he lets people take advantage of his relaxed nature to "bowl him over" and take over his social situations without regard to what he really wants.

Because of that, he doesn't see himself as somebody respectable. It's not easy to reach this point just from analyzing a reaction to an interruption, but that's how you come to the point of understanding and changing your core beliefs.

Finding Alternate Beliefs

Now you've gotten to the bottom of your situation and figured out what your core beliefs are. This is the exact moment to start challenging these very beliefs and wearing a new groove. It's a process in which you admit that your belief was wrong and replace it with a more realistic or helpful belief.

The first step is writing down one of the beliefs you've just uncovered. Ask yourself what experiences you've had that prove your belief wasn't always true. Generate as many experiences as you can and be very specific about what happened. Don't worry if you're not entirely sure these experiences were totally applicable—just list them all.

Using these past experiences as a guide, you can now produce a more balanced, healthier core belief that will hopefully replace the one that's been the source of your distress. Let's take Steve's core belief from above: that he doesn't deserve respect. He writes that down on a piece of paper.

He tries to remember times when he *did* earn respect. He remembers when he was in college and was viewed as a great philosophy student. Classmates seemed to like his answers and asked him for help in understanding their coursework. On a social level, Steve remembers a few times when he was appreciated for giving sound advice to friends who needed help, how many times they laughed at his jokes, and how clever they thought he was.

There you go, Stevie boy! You *do* have a track record of respect. People like you and want to hear you out. Sometimes other people aren't aware of boundaries, but that's their issue—and not a reflection of how much respect you deserve. When you can find a whole boatload of evidence to the contrary of your negative core belief—an inevitability—then it almost can't be argued with. Emotionally, you may still identify with the negative core belief, but little by little, you can accept a different story about yourself—the truth.

Steve's new belief might go something like this: "I deserve and have earned respect in the past. I just need to remember that sometimes other people aren't entirely aware of my situation, and it's not a reflection on me or my deserving to be respected. I have nothing to fear from those types of situations."

That's the long, complex, tedious process of changing your no response into a yes response. It requires proactively recognizing that we are inherently wired to say "no" more often than not and redirecting your neural pathways to allow you to overcome fear and anxiety. It can be as simple as walking to the edge of a tall building repeatedly to build the association that heights are safe and thus dig the neural groove. It can be what Stevie did in challenging his social fears. Whatever the case, it should be clear that the neuroscience of yes and no is, like everything else, dictated by the simple patterns we are exposed to.

Takeaways:

- This chapter is about the neuroscience of why we are compelled to say yes or no. When we say yes, we are allowing our intentions to translate directly into action. When we say no, we are holding ourselves back, and a rift opens between the intention and action. This concerns neuroplasticity because, as with everything else, these responses wear grooves over time and cause physical changes in the brain. This is a type of structural neuroplasticity as it involves neurotransmitters being released more/less over a period of time.

- The yes response concerns motivation, self-discipline, and the ability to achieve what we want. It is predicated on dopamine, which is generally the neurotransmitter associated with pleasure. If you can delay your compulsion for dopamine, you can accomplish what you want. That's the neural groove you want to build. There is also a brain inhibition system that helps us focus and deal with distractions, which is another muscle to practice flexing.

- Finally, with regards to the yes response, the brain doesn't differentiate between real and imagined events. This means that talking to yourself and visualizing future outcomes allows you to build your yes response without even having to lift a finger. You can experience physical changes in the brain without physical activity.

- As for the no response, it is all predicated on fear, anxiety, and the fact that our brains think it is still 10,000 BC with all the associated survival instincts. The fight-or-flight instinct makes us say no and self-sabotage more often than not. It prioritizes immediate action and/or pleasure over all else, which understandably makes it difficult to logically say yes when your entire body is irrationally and emotionally insisting that you must fight or flee. It is more powerful than the yes response because the overarching goal is urgent survival.

- The way to overcome the no response and overcome your fears, essentially, is a process called cognitive behavioral therapy. It consists of understanding what triggered your no responses, analyzing them, and then consciously (and painfully) constructing a yes response.

Chapter 5. Creating and Breaking Unconscious Habits

There may be no better example of neuroplasticity in action than the formation of habits—for better and worse. Because of this, you might even feel that there is slight repetition in this chapter because we have covered some of these aspects of neuroplasticity in earlier chapters.

With every repetitive act that we make, our neural pathways get reinforced and restructured until they become automatic channels that dictate what we do. Habits organize our neurons in a way that some actions become second nature (biting your nails), while others become nearly impossible to execute (*not* biting your nails).

Habits of course can be good or negative, and they are simply a reflection of what we are repeatedly exposed to. After all, the brain doesn't discriminate; it just follows what it sees. This is something we'll explore later on in the context of addiction.

Novel circumstances won't make an imprint on the brain because there's no telling if they will arise again. In other words, the brain isn't sure this knowledge will be useful in the future, so it's on a "wait and see" basis. However, the brain is quick to habituate and make things more speedy and efficient for the future. So when a circumstance or piece of information keeps coming up, the brain takes notice and immediately begins to wear a groove to make things easier in the future. Grooves form based on time, not benefit to you.

Picture an investigative journalist. She has years of experience in intense research. She's dogged about not leaving any stone unturned. She's met and interviewed thousands of experts and has operated on strict deadlines. She's a heavy reader and an avid learner. And she's extremely methodical about everything else in her life—she sticks to a reasonable diet and doesn't smoke or drink to excess.

This sounds like a fairly disciplined person, but it would be a mistake to say that she was disciplined right when she started her career.

All of these traits come from years of fashioning certain appropriate habits in her life and work. The more time she's spent on them, the more her brain has modified itself to adjust to her accomplishments. Everything that sounds impressive about the journalist has become second nature by way of neuroplasticity. Most of her functionality is automatic, and her resistance to outside substances that might throw her off course is strong and effortless.

Picture how you began to recognize all of the milestones and steps in your commute to your job or office. It wasn't immediate, and it took time. But once you started repeating the journey, your brain took notice and soon you could not pay attention and still arrive intact.

Habits and the Brain

There are two structures of the brain that are especially active in the formation of habits: the orbitofrontal cortex, located in the frontal lobe, and the striatum, a small organ near the center of the brain that's part of the basal ganglia. We've touched on these structures before, but it's time to dive into deeper detail about just how they affect habits.

The orbitofrontal cortex is a major player in the act of decision-making, whereas the striatum coordinates planning of motor activities, rewards, and repetitive behaviors, among other things. The orbitofrontal cortex is where our brain processes what we're going to do. People suffering damage to the orbitofrontal cortex are often described as impulsive. The most famous example is Phineas Gage.

Impulsivity involves behaviors that are inappropriate for the context, premature, poorly planned, and often result in adverse consequences—in other words, the opposite of habits. There is a constant struggle to meet a certain goal versus the desire to indulge in what's comfortable, familiar, easy, safe, and lazy. The latter is habitual behavior.

These parts are impossible to discuss alone because one begets the other. As conscious decisions are repeatedly made in the orbitofrontal cortex, they become engraved in the striatum. They are two parts of the same machine. It can help you to imagine these two parts in the following manner: the orbitofrontal cortex is the *thinking* part, whereas the striatum is the *doing* part.

Research on the striatum revealed that the sequence of neural firing goes through a certain alteration in the process of forming a habit. MIT professor Ann Graybiel conducted a series of tests on rats in a maze. The animals were "taught" to turn left or right upon the issuance of a certain tone.

When the rats were starting a certain task, the neurons in their brains fired through the entire sequence of the task. But as they repeated the task and built up a habit, the neurons fired only at the beginning and at the completion of their work. After eliminating other causes, Graybiel confirmed that the synaptic firings only occurred before the task was begun and after the task was finished.

In short, the brain was taught to "believe" that the entire chain of events in rats navigating the maze (step in, run around, turn left, turn right, turn left again, turn right, run through the exit) had essentially been chunked as *two* events (step in maze, exit maze). This finding revealed a lot about how habits are formed and how little mental energy is required to perform them. We go into autopilot and that's a sign of how deep neural grooves can be worn.

Another team at Duke University studied neural activity in the brain by training mice to press a lever to get a treat. The research team began by getting a group of healthy mice hooked on sugar. Similar to classic studies on drug addiction, the mice in this study were trained to press a tiny lever to receive doses of sweets. Once the mice were hooked, they continued pressing the lever even when the sweets were removed. For a human parallel, imagine when a smoker tries to give up smoking but still has to occupy his mouth with gum or a toothpick.

That was step one: establishing a behavioral pattern to get the goods.

Then the researchers compared the brains of the sugar-dependent mice to another group of healthy mice not hooked on sugar, focusing particularly on the network of brain areas known as the basal ganglia. In studies of drug addiction, electrical activity in this brain network is traceable along two main pathways: one that carries a "go" signal, which triggers action to pursue the object of the addiction, and one that carries a "stop" signal, which puts the brakes on the pursuit. It's the give and take between these pathways that regulates how we pursue just about anything.

In the brains of the mice hooked on sugar, the researchers found stronger, more active go and stop signals than in the mice not hooked on sugar. And they found that in the sugar-dependent group, the go signal consistently appeared before the stop signal. In the non-dependent group, the stop signal appeared before the go signal. In other words, the brains of the sugar-hooked mice lost the braking capacity to regulate their behavior.

This tells us that once a behavioral pattern was established and reinforced (pressing the lever to get more sugar), the brains of the mice changed in a significant and enduring way. Both "stop" and "go" signals in their basal ganglia networks became hyper-charged, but they also flipped, with the go signal bumping out the stop signal.

The result of those changes is that the mice continued pursuing sugar even when it was gone. The circuitry changes in their brains produced a strong signal to get more sweets. We humans call that signal a craving. Filling the craving reinforces the very system that's propelling the brain to want more, and thus a habit is born. It's the feeling that you simply feel discomfort when sleeping without brushing your teeth or walking out the door without turning your lights off.

At the same time, the brain produces a neurochemical called endocannabinoid, which reduces the activity of neurons in general. And you know from the prior studies that the less activity, the more habitual behavior will occur. These inhibitors therefore make it much easier for people to develop habits (and harder to break them) and otherwise fall into routine patterns of behavior that slowly become subconscious and prey to following the neural groove that has been set.

These studies reveal how the brain ultimately hard-wires itself to form habits. By consolidating a sequence of behaviors into one and firing certain neurons that compel someone to start an activity, habits become almost automated in the brain.

Hebb's Axiom

The entire school of thought about habits and neuroplasticity is centered around Hebbian theory, named after its inventor, neuroscientist David Hebb. Word for word, Hebb's axiom states the following:

> *When an axon of cell A is near enough to excite a cell B and repeatedly or persistently takes part in firing it, some growth process or metabolic change takes place in one or both cells such that A's efficiency, as one of the cells firing B, is increased.*

Put more simply, "cells that wire together, fire together." If a group of cells tends to light up together over an extended period of time, the more consistently and frequently they'll continue to do so. One of the cells has to fire *first*, of course. But the more constantly that closely related cells interact, the more they become fused in a neural sense and the faster they'll get as time goes on. Each decision you make is important from the cumulative standpoint.

Habits form as a result of this process—both positive and negative ones. Someone who constantly engages in harmful or broken behavior will likely develop more similarly dysfunctional habits. The neural pathways involved get reinforced and redoubled, and that results in patterns of behavior that aren't always beneficial. Also, remember the "use it or lose it" axiom: if certain neural pathways don't get used, the brain eventually filters them out, including those that encourage positive behavior.

The news isn't all bad. Like any form of training, whether it's physical or educational, neural pathways and grouping neurons together associated with positive behavior can be built over time. That also goes for personality traits one might consider inflexible or unable to change. Since the brain maintains a state of plasticity even into adulthood, there's always the possibility that it can be manipulated in a good way to develop beneficial habits.

Not *all* personality traits can be changed, of course, and even the ones that can require time and effort. But British psychologists from the University of Manchester identified five aspects of personality that *can* be altered or built over a period of time: openness to experience, conscientiousness, extroversion, agreeableness, and neuroticism. These factors are especially subject to change according to our life experiences—graduating college, getting and losing a job, getting married and breaking up, and so forth.

Your brain changes according to what it's most familiar with—what happens the most in your life. Someone who works on an assembly line is going to have a brain that's wired differently than a globe-trotting diplomat. Their causal networks are simply fashioned after a different set of experiences. But we also control that reality through the decisions and directions we take ourselves. That's why each decision you make needs to be carefully considered; every single one is important. For neuroplasticity to take effect the way we want it to, consistency is the key.

Addiction and Neuroplasticity

Being as malleable as it is, the brain can be conditioned to effect behavioral habits both good and bad. One unfavorable outcome is substance addiction. But one can use their understanding of how the addict mind "works" to bring about changes that are positive. Initially, it's done by hijacking the release of dopamine, the neurotransmitter we've discussed that is most associated with feelings of pleasure. After that, we see familiar patterns of neuroplasticity grooves that are hard to escape once they are set.

The dopamine system includes the neural pathways the brain uses for basic survival. We do whatever it is we need to maintain existence—eat, exercise, sleep, socialize. When the demand we're filling gets met, the brain is flooded with dopamine. In this way, nature is teaching us what survival requires and incentivizes us to seek it out when we may not always be aware of what we need. It also encourages us to do that thing again at our next convenience, sooner better than later. Dopamine quickly becomes associated with pleasure, and for some of us, pursuing that pleasure becomes all-consuming.

Addicts, for instance. Certain substances trigger a massive release of dopamine— anywhere from two to ten times more than the amount "natural" rewards stimulate— and do it more quickly and dependably. The hippocampus remembers how fantastic the drug felt, the amygdala takes note of what "cued" or triggered that use, and the prefrontal cortex becomes a one-track hunter who wants to locate that substance whatever the cost. Combine that with some people's genetic tendency to be more sensitive to dopamine or release more than average already, and you have the ingredients of an addict.

The addict becomes drawn to whatever substance can produce the release more strongly, acutely, and reliably. But after a number of times the brain begins to build tolerance for the substance, and in time the dopamine release starts to taper off. What worked the first time won't work again, so the addict needs to up the original dosage to the point where that dopamine release is effective enough to be pleasurable.

And then, of course, the brain's neural pathways have become so entrenched that it triggers withdrawal symptoms; the addict needs to take an extremely high dosage of the substance just to stop the shakes. From there, the downward spiral commences. That's the first way that addiction can change a brain.

The second way is simply how these neural grooves become entrenched in someone's brain, and it becomes a perpetual state of mind to have drugs on the mind, seek dopamine, and grow the habit of seeking out release. Remember Hebb's axiom and how it applies here—cells that fire together wire together, so this entire sequence becomes something that is familiar and psychologically sought after.

This is a tough place to dig oneself out of. It requires good decisions on a consistent basis. Recall that the brain doesn't always differentiate between imagining you're doing something and actually doing it. The neural pathways get etched with your *thoughts* of practicing just the same as with physical practice. This means it even requires good *thoughts* on a consistent basis.

And then you'd do this over and over so that your neural pathways get completely rewired.

How to Build (or Break) Habits

The habit loop is the neurological circuit that rules all the habits we develop. The brain is always trying to make everything it does more time-efficient and productive. To that end, it tries to turn as many things into habits as it possibly can, because they then become quicker and easier to execute so the brain can work on other things. Remember how, with habits, neurons only fire at the beginning and the end of any given execution? That's how it happens—there's less brain energy involved when a behavior gets to that point, and the neural network can start "chunking."

Since this whole process happens on a subconscious (or *un*conscious) level, the habit loop can result in both good and bad behaviors. To change the habit, one must be more aware and take direct action with the habit loop and understand exactly what happens at each stage of it. Neuroplasticity sometimes happens too easily. What follows is a helpful guideline, as put forth by author Charles Duhigg, on how to take control of how your neural connections are wired.

There are three stages: the cue, routine, and reward.

The cue. Habits are generally triggered by something that tells the brain to go into "instant gratification" mode. It's not always a preceding event, though it certainly can be. It can also be set off by being in a particular locale or at a certain time of the day. One's current emotional state can trigger the behavior, as can other people's actions or words. For example, a typical emotional state that triggers behavior is stress. If you feel stress, you might pick at your hair or bite your nails. A more sinister example would be self-medicating with alcohol when stressed in an attempt to dull the anxiety.

The routine. This is the behavior you're looking to change—whether it's something you want to quit or something you want to start doing. Your routine when stressed might be to start smoking, or you might want to introduce the routine of taking daily walks around the park after dinner. The routine is really what the habit is, and it's important to understand that it doesn't exist in a vacuum and indeed doesn't even occur consciously or out of free will. In the case of bad habits, it all stems from a cue. In the case of good habits, we must proactively and consciously associate it with a cue.

The reward. What do you get from the habit you want to break? Or what do you *want to* get from a new routine? The reward is the reason your brain remembers how to get what it wants, whether it's tangible or intangible. It could be the momentary release from stress and anxiety. It could be the taste of cheese puffs on your tongue, a jolt of energy from a triple espresso, or a happy feeling from a night out with friends. Of course, for addicts, the reward is either euphoria or just getting back to feeling "normal." But for the rest of us, this is a subtle incentive that, over time, builds the groove of neuroplasticity and cements our behavioral patterns.

To break bad habits and build good ones and rewire your brain in the way that you want, you must be hyper-cognizant of each step in the habit loop and comprehend it fully, then work with it on a conscious level to tweak the routine and reward stages. Done over a committed period of time, this process will help strengthen the neural pathways that lead to desired behaviors and hopefully de-emphasize the ones that don't.

Identify the routine. What concrete activity do you want to change? You might want to stop smoking. You might want to start exercising. You might want to cut down on sugary snacks. You might want to *start* drinking two liters of water a day. Know what your end goal is, because that influences the rest of the process.

Experiment with the reward system. This will probably take up the most time out of any part of this process. For a habit you want to break or create, consider *why* you're really doing it. You might think you're drinking alcohol just to get to sleep or to relieve stress, but you might also be self-medicating to avoid a kind of emotional pain. This is your motivation, and it requires looking inward and analyzing what you want out of a situation.

If you're seeking to become healthier by taking up an exercise routine, your reward and motivation might be getting in better physical shape. But other more specific benefits might take hold as well—you might feel quicker, more agile, more energetic, maybe even easier to be around in social settings. *And then* it might go a level deeper in terms of increasing your self-esteem and dealing with issues of social and romantic rejection. Thinking of the *bonus* rewards beyond your original one can do wonders for your motivation.

Isolate the cue or trigger. What's happening at the exact moment that you're feeling the urge to partake in a habit you're trying to break? What happens right as you reach for the bottle or bring your hand to your mouth for a chewing session?

Answer these questions as they correspond to these five different cues: where are you located, what time is it, who are you with, how do you feel, and what happens just before the urge comes upon you? Answer these questions as fully as you can. This goes for whether you're trying to change a habit or acquire one. You want to move from the state of one routine to a superior routine—so you either ask what's triggering your doing something unhelpful or discouraging you from doing something beneficial.

Plan how to obtain your reward in a desirable way. Think back to your experiments with the reward system: how do you get the benefits or relief you want in a healthy, supportive way? For example, if you're drinking to relieve stress and get to sleep, how else can you achieve those goals without picking up a bottle? You might want to take up meditation for the stress and get physical exercise to restore your sleeping patterns.

This part won't be easy, and it certainly won't be automatic. That's why the *planning* is important: knowing full well that it's a major operation and not just a small tweak, you'll hopefully be content with chipping away at the reward system's established patterns. It'll be easier for some than others, but it's not going to be an instant cakewalk for anybody. But everybody *can* do it.

This last step is really where neuroplasticity comes into play—you are seeking to purposefully rewire the neural connections that have been set and create new ones that aren't so easy as seeking immediate gratification.

Let's take two examples of how this loop might work: one for breaking a bad habit and another for acquiring a good one. We'll start with an example of someone wanting to cut down on junk food or quit altogether.

Identify the routine. Obviously, it's eating junk food. But get specific about it. What specific junk food are they gorging too much on: cheese curls, ice cream, deep-dish pizza? They'd also want to think about what happens directly before they start eating: how do they approach it, and how do they feel afterward?

Experiment with the reward system. There are several payoffs to eating junk food. It satisfies a craving; it answers a desire for something that tastes good. The texture, the smell, the residue of cheese dust it leaves on the tongue. So how can they channel those desires into food that's healthier? We'll figure that out in the planning stage, but next...

Isolate the cue. Anything can trigger a junk food binge, but for this example let's say there are two prompts: boredom and anxiety. If there's nothing going on that's interesting in the house, they alleviate that sense of boredom by tearing into a pound cake. Or if they're caught in a stressful situation or dreading something that may be happening in the future, they'll mollify those fears by ripping into a plate of nachos. Now that they've figured out how the routine gets called out, it's easier to diagnose and plan for alternate courses of action.

Plan how to obtain the reward in a healthy way. First, they'd devise a plan of action on how to deal with boredom and anxiety: take on a hobby or a distraction for the boredom and try to adopt meditative techniques for the anxiety. Then there's the matter of planning the healthier reward, which they can do by researching slightly healthier versions of the junk food they're eating—at the very least they could find some organic substitutes. They could also learn how to cook their own food by experimenting with spices and other natural elements that could widen their palette and satisfy certain cravings. Long-term, they could envision the reward of being healthier and more energetic.

Now let's take on someone who wants to *obtain* a habit: someone who wants to develop strong reading habits. In this model, we follow the same steps as someone who wants to break a habit, but we may do a little reverse engineering in a couple of instances.

Identify the routine. What does the person want to do? Read for comprehension. Be fearless about reading everything: fiction, non-fiction, poetry, autobiographies, even long reports with lots of numbers if they felt like it.

Experiment with the reward system. What do they imagine the benefits of reading are? They'll be better informed, for one thing. They'll have a firmer grasp on some of the themes of great literature, possibly. They'll be entertained or amused in a relatively harmless way. And they may even find inspiration to write something themselves.

Isolate the cue. This is a little bit different than the breaking-the-habit scenario, because we're trying to find cues for something the prospective book-reader *wants* to do on a habitual basis. So perhaps a more accurate question is this: what are the forces at work right now, before the habit has been developed, that are making them want to read more? It could be intellectual insecurity, the feeling like they're ignorant or stupid. They might also be afraid that they won't understand everything they read. They might be jealous of people who seem to be well-read and can quote written work endlessly. Or they may be burned out on TV, the Internet, and video games and have a yearning for something more fulfilling.

Plan how to obtain the reward in a healthy way. There's no really *unhealthy* way to read, but there are practical steps on how to go about it that might make it easier. A good part of this strategy will work off the various insecurities in the "cue" section. First, maybe they'd want to unplug their TV and computer. Then they'd want to be accepting of their estimation of their reading level and give themselves permission to start off with a book suited to their reading level. They'd understand this is the beginning of an intellectual renaissance, not the result of stupidity.

They could develop a system for taking notes on what they're reading and keep a list of terms or subjects they need to know more about. They could also block out a certain amount of time every day for reading and stick to it. They could keep a journal about their thoughts and feelings about their reading materials. As they go along, they could incrementally increase the difficulty and depth of what they read. They could choose to read some books for information and others for plain old enjoyment.

And then, you know the rest. Wire your brain over time, frequency, and repetition. There's no shortcut.

Phillippa Lally, a health psychology researcher at University College London, published a study in the *European Journal of Social Psychology* that aimed to find out just how long the process of habit formation really takes. The study was conducted over the course of 12 weeks and examined the behavior of 96 participants who chose habits that they would try to build and then reported daily on how automatic the behavior felt. After analyzing the data, Lally and her team determined that, on average, it took 66 days for a daily action to become automatic.

How long it takes you to develop a new habit will depend on your existing habits and behavior as well as your personal circumstances. The quickest habit in Lally's study was developed in only 18 days, while the slowest took 254 days. Once you make it through the gauntlet, your habit will drive you to achieve where you used to require exercising self-discipline.

The If-Then Technique

A helpful technique that directly deals with the relationship between the cue and the routine as described in Duhigg's habit loop is the if-then technique. This is also sometimes known as an *implementation intention*—in other words, making your intention easy to implement. The *if* portion corresponds to the cue, while the *then* portion corresponds to the routine.

The simple fact is that there's a big gap between knowing what you want to do and actually getting it done. Whatever the case—distractions, inefficiencies, or procrastination—wearing neural grooves through consistent action will make it easier.

If-then statements take the following form: if X happens, then I will do Y. That's it. This is something you decide in advance, and there are two primary ways to use it. This makes it easier to build habits because all you have to do is plug your desired action in as a natural consequence of something that is certain to happen. When actions are chained and given forethought, they tend to happen.

As a quick example, *if* it is 3:00 p.m. on Sunday, *then* you will call your mother. Or more specific to habits you might want to cultivate, *if* it is 3:00 p.m., *then* you will drink two liters of water, or if it is 9:00 p.m., then you will floss your teeth. These are examples of when you use if-then to accomplish a specific goal, the first type of use. X can be whatever event, time, or occurrence you choose that happens on a daily basis, and Y is the specific action that you will take.

The if-then statement simply takes your goals and desired habits out of the ether and ties them to concrete moments in your day. A habit to eat healthier and drink more water has a set prescription, for instance, or a vow to have better dental health is carried out every day because it is contingent upon a daily occurrence. Instead of generalities, you get a time and place for when to act.

It seems simplistic, and it is, but it has been shown that you are two to three times more likely to succeed if you use an if-then plan than if you don't. In one study, 91% of people who used an if-then plan stuck to an exercise program versus 39% of non-planners. Peter Gollwitzer, the NYU psychologist who first articulated the power of if-then planning, recently reviewed results from 94 studies that used the technique and found significantly higher success rates for just about every goal you can think of, from using public transportation more frequently to avoiding stereotypical and prejudicial thoughts.

As you can imagine, this perceived lack of choice makes it easier to create the neuroplasticity you want—because there are no other paths. In a sense, it is like constructing an enriched environment for your mind because it leaves you with only one outcome, and thus the neural connections are forced to grow.

The primary reason if-then statements work so well is because they speak the language of your brain, which is the language of contingencies. Humans are good at encoding information in "If X, then Y" terms and using this process (often unconsciously) to guide our behavior. It's the basis of decision-making, which is often subconscious and instantaneous. The brain works by evaluating pros and cons, and it often happens in the limbic system without our recognition. That's the type of process we are intentionally creating.

Deciding exactly when and where you will act on your goal creates a link in your brain between the situation or cue (the *if*) and the behavior that should follow (the *then*).

Let's say your significant other has been giving you a hard time about forgetting to text to inform them that you will be working late and not make dinner. So you make an if-then plan: if it is 6:00 p.m. and I'm at work, then I will text my significant other. Now the situation "6:00 p.m. at work" is wired in your brain directly to the action "text my sugar bear."

Then the situation or cue "6:00 p.m. at work" becomes highly activated. Below your awareness, your brain starts scanning the environment, searching for the situation in the "if" part of your plan. Once the "if" part of your plan happens, the "then" part follows *automatically*. You don't *have* to consciously monitor your goal, which means your plans get carried out even when you are preoccupied.

The best part is that by detecting situations and directing behavior without conscious effort, if-then plans are far less taxing and require less willpower than mere resolutions. They enable us to conserve our self-discipline for when it's really needed and compensate for it when we don't have enough. Armed with if-thens, you can tell your fickle friend willpower that this year, you really won't be needing him.

The second use is also related to achieving a specific goal, but rather it's how to avoid *failing* at that goal. You would still use if X then Y, but X would be an unexpected situation that you want to maintain control in and deal with. In the first use, X is simply any everyday situation, occurrence, or event. Here, X is something that may not happen but you want to be prepared for. For instance, if you want to create a habit of drinking water, *if* you eat out at a restaurant, *then* you will get water with lemon only. That's a situation that isn't certain to occur, but it helps you adhere to your habit from the opposite end.

Complete these statements *before* you are in a dire situation and you can see how they work for you. It is like creating a rule for yourself to abide by. If you've given it thought beforehand, you can default to that guideline and not have to try to make a risky decision in the heat of the moment.

Anticipate what's to happen and you are a step ahead of the game.

As another example, suppose it's your birthday, but you're on a strict diet and your office has a thing for surprise parties so you'll probably be getting one. "If they brought cake, then I'll turn it down and immediately drink a big glass of water." Alternatively, you could be having a problem with procrastination, and you're settling in for a big project you have to finish. You could say, "If the phone rings, then I'll ignore it until I'm done."

You can get more detailed with these statements and can prepare them for situations with more significance or danger than the above examples. But whatever the case, the if-then method forces you to project yourself into common scenarios that could trigger reversion to your bad habits—and makes you plan for those triggers. It takes away your residuals of false justification and excuses for doing the wrong thing (or doing nothing) and sharpens your commitment to meeting your goals.

All of these methods help focus on the minute but powerful triggers that lead us into the personal infractions we're trying to eliminate, and they help defray the residual personal reactions that arise from forcing change in our lives. Best of all, they don't rely on sweeping or exhaustive changes to who we are—they make our brains and natural impulses work *for* us instead of going to sleep on the job.

Once again, deciding exactly how you'll react to circumstances regarding your goal creates a link in your brain between the situation or cue (if) and the behavior that should follow (then.) And as we know, everything good that we want happens in our brain.

Common Pitfalls to Habit Formation

This chapter has thus far been dedicated to ensuring that habitual behaviors, as driven by the orbitofrontal cortex and the striatum, are occurring consistently and strategically. But there's another side to that—avoiding the pitfalls that will cause your neuroplasticity to essentially be all over the map, producing multiple grooves, none of which are particularly helpful to you. They are common, and they prevent anything useful from being neutrally encoded.

If we take the same example of wanting to build the habit of drinking more water, it takes a while for conscious decisions to become ingrained as a natural instinct. It requires purposeful repetition. You might instead have built a hazy habit to quench your thirst with soda or mistake your thirst or hunger. To get the exact habit you desire, we have to be exact about the process we use.

One of the primary sources for a framework on pitfalls in behavior change is B.J. Fogg, a researcher from Stanford University. His expertise is in the scientific basis of behavior change and habits, and he articulated 10 major mistakes in attempting to change one's behavior. We'll focus on just a few of them as they relate to neuroplasticity and brain training.

Attempting big leaps instead of baby steps. We tend to focus on change as an overwhelming major event—not a series of smaller steps that lead practically to a positive solution. We celebrate when a baseball team wins the World Series, not when they win the first game of spring training. We only think about the end product, no matter how grand it is, and prefer to gloss over the small steps that make up that end product.

That view undermines the truth that it takes a lot of smaller work for change to be successful, and it can distort our strategy. We feel underwhelmed and discouraged when we've lost only one pound over the course of a week or when we don't have complete knowledge of a school subject after reading the material only once.

Fogg urges us to focus on the smaller picture and celebrate the miniature progress we make step by step. Realizing the larger goal is fine, but building new behaviors relies on the accumulation of small acts, each of which encourages you, builds your neural groove, and tells you it's okay to go even further next time. Everything starts with something small, and sometimes it's hard to see how it can contribute to the end goal—but they can and do.

If habits are built upon consistency, then the best thing you can do is make consistency easy. That means starting small and prioritizing simply taking action over all else. If you're out of shape and want to get fit, start with taking a 20-minute walk every day rather than immediately jumping into a workout routine that will make you sore and miserable. Start with five minutes, even.

Trying to stop old behaviors instead of creating new ones. Successfully stopping a bad habit by going "cold turkey" is more the exception than the rule. We make vows to stop smoking or drinking by shutting consumption down completely. But this frequently fails because we haven't come up with an answer for the cravings we feel; we've just told ourselves we're going to deal with the discomfort without knowing how. Your brain is still expecting to be satisfied with the behavior you're cutting off, and your brain is not happy about this. We know this from the habit loop we've discussed and how our compulsions will keep running down the same neural grooves in the absence of anything else.

The solution is to replace the old behavior or routine with a new one—but one that delivers some kind of compensatory reward that the brain can understand. Stopping a bad habit is less effective than creating a new one to replace it.

If you're trying to give up sugary sweets but your brain craves the reward, try eating a piece of healthy fruit. If you're craving a cigarette, try finding a motor activity—playing piano, housecleaning, or building furniture—that gives you a sense of accomplishment. Simply telling someone to stop indulging is tough; replacing that feeling is both more productive and sustainable.

Believing that information alone leads to action. I hope you've enjoyed this book and that it gave you a lot of valuable information. But you're not done, even though this book nearly is.

Knowing the facts about a certain situation does not equal working on it. You can tell someone why it's important to stop smoking, exercise, or increase their attention span, but that's not sufficient stimuli in and of itself. The passive absorption of information does nothing to your brain structures, though it's important to note that talking to yourself and visualizing that information in action *does* make a difference.

Instead of gathering more intelligence on what you need to do, begin applying the information in real situations. Focus on identifying your triggers, adjusting your patterns, putting effort into it, and recording your results on a regular basis. Information alone won't get you where you want to be; it's only when your brain is actively engaged that habits are formed.

Additionally, as Mike Tyson once said, *"Everyone has a plan until they get punched in the face."* Your plans, based on all the information you've gathered, might be useless once you start and realize they won't work for you. Therefore, action is paramount. Leap before you look occasionally.

Seeking to change a behavior forever, not for a short time. This is similar to the first of Fogg's flaws we discussed—trying to make large changes instead of small ones. Instead of the *size* of the change, this failing concerns the *time* element. Making overly ambitious proclamations that we'll banish the bad and embrace the good until the end of time distorts the reality of change— again, that it's the culmination of several small changes executed faithfully over an extended period of time. This is why 12-step programs focus on the "now" and tracking progress "one day at a time." There is too much of an emphasis on the end result otherwise, and that leads to disappointment and discouragement.

The solution to this problem is at least a little obvious: limit the range of time you're focusing on and accept the accomplishment of changing on a smaller scale and a day-by-day frame of mind.

Writer and author James Clear phrases this flaw in behavior change similarly. He calls it seeking a result rather than a ritual.

He notes that we tend to value the payoff and outcome in contemporary society. We're looking to lose 100 pounds, increase our productivity by 110%, finish first in the marathon, and, if we have time, stave off death forever. We may value effort, but if it doesn't produce the results we want exactly as we want them, we consider that effort to have failed. The problem with this, Clear says, is that "New goals don't deliver new results. New lifestyles do." For this reason, he suggests envisioning behavior change as something that happens every day—as a ritual.

Over time and repetition, these rituals add up and produce solid lifestyle changes. It may be frustrating that we don't see immediate effects from a day or two of changing behavior. But we can gauge progress more incrementally—after a year, a month, or even a week.

The trick is putting your thoughts, emotions, and efforts into keeping the ritual. Focus on the 15-minute jog, the 20 minutes of meditation, the 30 minutes of studying, or the hour of music practice that you repeat every day. You can refine or add to those rituals as you keep them up—but keep your mind oriented on the routine in and of itself.

Takeaways:

- If you want the clearest illustration of neuroplasticity, look no further than habits. Habits are conscious decisions and actions that, over time, become instinctual and automatic. Neuroplasticity in general is governed by what's known as Hebb's axiom, which essentially states that "cells that fire together wire together." This, of course, is a primary aspect of structural neuroplasticity and the strengthening of neuronal connections. Of course, there is a biological basis to it, which primarily concerns two brain structures: the orbitofrontal cortex and the striatum.

- Unfortunately, Hebb's axiom isn't solely a force for good. Since habits form solelybased on what the brain is exposed to, a bad habit is just as easy to form as a good habit. This also means that addiction and substance abuse have their origins in the brain's capacity for adaptation and change.

- If habits are built through consistent action over time, then it's imperative that we understand how to make being consistent easy. This is embodied in Charles Duhigg's habit loop, which consists of a cue, routine, and reward. It requires you to examine each element of a habit and carefully tailor them to your desires. After all, you don't want the wrong neural groove to rule the day.

- The if-then technique allows you to make decisions beforehand in a way that your mind likes to operate: contingencies. It generally takes the form of "If X occurs, then I will do Y." It can be used to bring you closer to your desired goals and habits by tying them to an everyday inevitability. It can also be used to protect against failure, to be used in a dire circumstance where your willpower might cave. This forces you to set guidelines and anticipate the hardships you may face. If-then allows you to avoid using willpower and discipline and build an automatic neural groove between an intent and an action.

- B.J. Fogg and James Clear articulate a few major pitfalls that can occur in habit formation; they mostly concern shooting for big steps rather than small, trying to stop old behaviors rather than start new ones, believing that information leads to change, and focusing on the outcome instead of on daily rituals and actions.

Summary Guide

Chapter 1. Neuroscience, Plasticity, and the Changing Brain

- What does it mean to build a better brain? Are our intelligence, functioning, and behaviors a result of our brains? In a nutshell, yes. Our brains are the center of who we are, and they dictate what we do even when we try to avoid it. Neuroplasticity is the process of the brain developing, changing, growing, and adapting to whatever it is exposed to, and it can be used to quite literally build a better brain.

- A couple of examples are stark illustrations of just how the brain can change, for better or for worse. Phineas Gage is a man who had an iron rod blown through a part of his brain. He lived and could still function as a relatively normal human being, albeit off-putting and fairly unpopular. This is because the iron rod tore through his prefrontal cortex, the portion of the brain responsible for personality and inhibition. This shows how the brain has separate structures for separate functions.

- Next, the phenomenon of phantom limbs is when amputees feel sensation or pain where their limbs used to be. This occurs because of cortical remapping, which is when adjacent parts of the brain take over parts that used to be used for the missing limb. This shows just how the brain compensates, heals itself, and changes physically.

- When it comes to specific brain structures, there are a few that we will focus on, as they relate to neuroplasticity and making changes. These include the prefrontal cortex, which is where conscious and analytical thought occurs; the limbic system, which is the emotional system that clashes with the prefrontal cortex; the hippocampus, where memory is processed; and the basal ganglia, where habits are formed and processed. Neuroplasticity is neutral, occurs in response to what it sees, and can be beneficial or detrimental.

- A helpful framework for understanding how neuroplasticity works is the triune brain theory. While not 100% correct and precise, it makes clear the forces at play in making neural changes. This theory states that there are three primary brains that are always at battle: the neomammalian (roughly corresponding to the prefrontal cortex), paleomammalian (roughly corresponding to the limbic system), and reptilian brain (roughly corresponding to the basal ganglia). The latter two brains are instinctual and subconscious, while changes made have to be conscious and thoughtful at first, so neuroplasticity depends on the ability of the neomammalian brain (prefrontal cortex) to win a certain percentage of the time.

Chapter 2. Plasticity in All Forms: How Does the Brain Change?

- What is neuroplasticity? We've perhaps danced around it, but we get down to the details here. It is the changes in your brain that are neutral by themselves and simply a reflection of our actions, thoughts, habits, environments, and so on.

- There are two types: structural and functional. Structural neuroplasticity concerns strengthening and creating neural connections over time, while functional is what happens when specific parts of the brain lose functionality and are compensated for by neighboring brain elements. Phantom limb sufferers who unknowingly utilize cortical remapping are using functional neuroplasticity, while learning new habits and information comes through structural changes.

- We mainly seek structural neuroplasticity for obvious reasons. One study in particular illustrates what neuroplasticity is all about: scientists have determined that animals that have been domesticated have smaller brains, and they've found that this finding also applies to human beings. Thus, neuroplasticity's changes aren't always positive or beneficial. That's why we must be proactive and intentional—the more challenge, discomfort, and effort spent, the more neuroplasticity will occur and the higher functioning our brains will be.

- Neuroplasticity was first thought to be impossible and then thought to be reserved only for children. Both of these notions were eventually proven wrong over time. Though we still suffer synaptic pruning throughout our lives, neuroplasticity also occurs throughout our lives, and neurogenesis has even been found in select portions of the brain, specifically those related to smell and memory—which, coincidentally, have been found to be related to each other. The brain changes and adapts only to what it experiences, and this is within our control.

Chapter 3. Principles of Neural Growth

- Neural growth is anything but easy. In fact, by definition, easy tasks don't really cause any growth. Think of the brain as the earth being shaped by rivers and lakes. Now that's a process that takes time and effort.
- Thus, the first principle to increasing neuroplasticity is about stimulation. You need more of it, as much as you can get in your daily life. Learning is one of the primary forms of mental stimulation. You essentially need to avoid passive activities and engage your brain and make it work.
- Second, enriched environments help create neuroplasticity because they offer you no other choice. Imagine being dropped into a foreign country—you would probably learn the language of that country pretty quickly out of necessity. Thus, there are specific ways in which you can design the various environments of your life to aid

stimulation and challenge. Not the most pleasant or comfortable way of living, but the most effective.

- Third, persistence and consistency. The Grand Canyon wasn't carved in a day, and neither will the neural connections that you wish to cultivate. To jump to yet another analogy, think of how you might approach a gym workout. You can have more sets, use heavier weights, go more frequently, or have a longer workout in general. Those are the ways that the brain grows as well.

- Fourth, the brain is not an ethereal entity. It has a physical basis for functioning, and it is mostly based on sleep, exercise, fuel, and stress (or the lack thereof). If you can't take care of your physical self, you can't expect your brain to perform very well.

Chapter 4. The Neuroscience of Yes and No

- This chapter is about the neuroscience of why we are compelled to say yes or no. When we say yes, we are allowing our intentions to translate directly into action. When we say no, we are holding ourselves back, and a rift opens between the intention and action. This concerns neuroplasticity because, as with everything else, these responses wear grooves over time and cause physical changes in the brain. This is a type of structural neuroplasticity as it involves neurotransmitters being released more/less over a period of time.

- The yes response concerns motivation, self-discipline, and the ability to achieve what we want. It is predicated on dopamine, which is generally the neurotransmitter associated with pleasure. If you can delay your compulsion for dopamine, you can accomplish what you want. That's the neural groove you want to build. There is also a brain inhibition system that helps us focus and deal with distractions, which is another muscle to practice flexing.

- Finally, with regards to the yes response, the brain doesn't differentiate between real and imagined events. This means that talking to yourself and visualizing future outcomes allows you to build your yes response without even having to lift a finger. You can experience physical changes in the brain without physical activity.

- As for the no response, it is all predicated on fear, anxiety, and the fact that our brains think it is still 10,000 BC with all the associated survival instincts. The fight-or-flight instinct makes us say no and self-sabotage more often than not. It prioritizes immediate action and/or pleasure over all else, which understandably makes it difficult to logically say yes when your entire body is irrationally and emotionally insisting that you must fight or flee. It is more powerful than the yes response because the overarching goal is urgent survival.

- The way to overcome the no response and overcome your fears, essentially, is a process called cognitive behavioral therapy. It consists of understanding what triggered your no responses, analyzing them, and then consciously

(and painfully) constructing a yes
response.

Chapter 5. Creating and Breaking Unconscious Habits

- If you want the clearest illustration of
  neuroplasticity, look no further than
  habits. Habits are conscious decisions
  and actions that, over time, become
  instinctual and automatic.
  Neuroplasticity in general is governed
  by what's known as Hebb's axiom, which
  essentially states that "cells that fire
  together wire together." This, of course,
  is a primary aspect of structural
  neuroplasticity and the strengthening of
  neuronal connections. Of course, there is
  a biological basis to it, which primarily
  concerns two brain structures: the
  orbitofrontal cortex and the striatum.

- Unfortunately, Hebb's axiom isn't solely
  a force for good. Since habits form
  solelybased on what the brain is
  exposed to, a bad habit is just as easy to
  form as a good habit. This also means
  that addiction and substance abuse have

their origins in the brain's capacity for adaptation and change.

- If habits are built through consistent action over time, then it's imperative that we understand how to make being consistent easy. This is embodied in Charles Duhigg's habit loop, which consists of a cue, routine, and reward. It requires you to examine each element of a habit and carefully tailor them to your desires. After all, you don't want the wrong neural groove to rule the day.

- The if-then technique allows you to make decisions beforehand in a way that your mind likes to operate: contingencies. It generally takes the form of "If X occurs, then I will do Y." It can be used to bring you closer to your desired goals and habits by tying them to an everyday inevitability. It can also be used to protect against failure, to be used in a dire circumstance where your willpower might cave. This forces you to set guidelines and anticipate the hardships you may face. If-then allows you to avoid using willpower and discipline and build an automatic neural groove between an intent and an action.

- B.J. Fogg and James Clear articulate a few major pitfalls that can occur in habit formation; they mostly concern shooting for big steps rather than small, trying to stop old behaviors rather than start new ones, believing that information leads to change, and focusing on the outcome instead of on daily rituals and actions.

Made in the USA
Columbia, SC
13 October 2020